The
Goddess Path

Secret Forms of the Goddess and
the Rituals of Resurrection

Mysticism of Ushet Rekhat

Mysticism of the Ancient Egyptian Goddess

On the Front Cover: Goddess Nut receiving offerings.
On the Back Cover: Goddess Hetheru

Cruzian Mystic Books
P.O.Box 570459
Miami, Florida, 33257
(305) 378-6253 Fax: (305) 378-6253

First U.S. edition 1996
Second Edition © 1997 By Reginald Muata Abhaya Ashby

Third Edition © 2001 By Reginald Muata Abhaya Ashby

The author is available for group lectures and individual counseling. For further information contact the publisher.

Ashby, Muata Dr.
The Goddess Path: Secret Forms of the Goddess and the Rituals of Resurrection
ISBN: 1-884564-18-6

Formerly: *Mysticism of Ushet Rekhat: Worship of the Goddess*

Library of Congress Cataloging in Publication Data

1 Goddess 2 Spirituality 3 Egyptian Mythology 4 Yoga 5 Self Help.
6 Egyptian Mysticism 7 African spirituality & Mysticism

Also by Muata Ashby

Egyptian Yoga: The Philosophy of Enlightenment.
Initiation Into Egyptian Yoga: The Secrets of Sheti.
Egyptian Proverbs: Tempt Tchaas.
The Egyptian Yoga Exercise Workout Book.

For a complete listing of titles send for the catalog in the back of the book.

Sema
Institute of Yoga

Sema (☥) is an ancient Egyptian word and symbol meaning *union*. The Sema Institute is dedicated to the propagation of the universal teachings of spiritual evolution which relate to the union of humanity and the union of all things within the universe. It is a non-denominational organization which recognizes the unifying principles in all spiritual and religious systems of evolution throughout the world. Our primary goals are to provide the wisdom of ancient spiritual teachings in books, courses and other forms of communication. Secondly, to provide expert instruction and training in the various yogic disciplines including Ancient Egyptian Philosophy, Christian Gnosticism, Indian Philosophy and modern science. Thirdly, to promote world peace and Universal Love.

A primary focus of our tradition is to identify and acknowledge the yogic principles within all religions and to relate them to each other in order to promote their deeper understanding as well as to show the essential unity of purpose and the unity of all living beings and nature within the whole of existence.

The Institute is open to all who believe in the principles of peace, non-violence and spiritual emancipation regardless of sex, race, or creed.

About the author and editor:
Dr. Muata Abhaya Ashby

About The Author

Reginald Muata Ashby holds a Doctor of Philosophy Degree in Religion, and a Doctor of Divinity Degree in Holistic Healing. He is also a Pastoral Counselor and Teacher of Yoga Philosophy and Discipline. Dr. Ashby is an adjunct faculty member of the American Institute of Holistic Theology and an ordained Minister. Dr. Ashby has studied advanced Jnana, Bhakti and Kundalini Yogas under the guidance of Swami Jyotirmayananda, a world renowned Yoga Master. He has studied the mystical teachings of ancient Egypt for many years and is the creator of the Egyptian Yoga concept. He is also the founder of the Sema Institute, an organization dedicated to the propagation of the teachings of Yoga and mystical spirituality.

Dr. Ashby began his research into the spiritual philosophy of Ancient Africa (Egypt) and India and noticed correlations in the culture and arts of the two countries. This was the catalyst for a successful book series on the subject called "Egyptian Yoga". Now he has created a series of musical compositions which explore this unique area of music from ancient Egypt and its connection to world music.

Karen Clarke-Ashby "Vijaya-Asha" is the wife and spiritual partner of Muata. She is an independent researcher, practitioner and certified teacher of Yoga, a Doctor in the Sciences and a Pastoral Counselor, the editor of Egyptian Proverbs and Egyptian Yoga by Muata.☥

Sema Institute
P.O. Box 570459, Miami, Fla. 33257 (305) 378-6253,
Fax (305) 378-6253
©1997-2001

Table of Contents

INTRODUCTION:
What is Ushet Rekhat?

The task of spiritual life is to reach enlightenment. Enlightenment is the term used to describe the highest level of spiritual awakening or consciousness where one experiences supreme peace and bliss. It means attaining such a level of spiritual awareness that one discovers the underlying unity of the entire universe, as well as the fact that the source of all Creation is the same source from which the innermost Self within every human heart arises. The journey of enlightenment implies getting closer to the Supreme Divinity, who is the source of all that exists. Therefore, the images and teachings of mystical wisdom are directed toward developing both an understanding of the Divine as well as a devotional feeling for the Divine. This two fold movement in reason and emotion leads the spiritual aspirant to discover his or her own innate Divinity through the integration of the whole personality.

In the movement to get close to the Divine, certain images, symbols and prayers are given by many religions. Sometimes the male image is given as the father and sometimes the female image is given as the mother. The father image gives the impression of a loving, compassionate, disciplinarian but is sometimes perceived as being somewhat distant and detached. The mother image gives more of an impression of closeness since a mother in human life is the closest being a child knows. The mother is the first person to be in contact with the child as they share the same body during the pregnancy period. After birth, the mother and child remain close as the mother nurses and nurtures the child. Thus, motherhood seems to imply a greater closeness than fatherhood, and this emotional content of the relationship is what devotional worship towards the Divine Mother emphasizes. As a closeness to the goddess develops, feelings of warmth and love emerge. These feelings are encouraged to evolve beyond a sentimental attachment to the image of the Goddess through the study of her wisdom teachings. The wisdom gradually leads to an unveiling of the goddess and the true nature of the Goddess becomes revealed in all her glory. This is known as the unveiling of Aset (Isis).

The Supreme Being may be worshipped as father or as mother. *Ushet Rekhat or Worship of the Goddess of Wisdom* is the spiritual process of worshipping the Divine in the form of the Goddess. It is based on the Ancient Egyptian teachings and it celebrates the most important forms of the goddess, including Aset, Maat, Arat, Amentet and Hetheru, while exploring their mystical meanings. The Divine Goddess implies the study of the star Sopdu (Sirius), the star of Aset (Isis), and the new birth of Hor or Heru (Horus). The Mother Worship devotional meditation ritual performed at the end of the year is based on the Ushet Rekhat. The end of the year is a time of reckoning and reflection. It is a time for engendering a new or renewed positive movement towards attaining spiritual enlightenment. During the ceremony, the cosmic forces, symbolized by the star Sopdu and the constellation Orion (Sahu), are harnessed through the understanding and devotional attitude of the participant. This propitiation draws the light of wisdom and health to all those who share in the ritual, leading to prosperity and expansion in consciousness.

7

Mysticism of the Ancient Egyptian Goddess

In Ancient Egypt, the Goddess was held in a special place among the symbols of Divinity. Perhaps in no other system of religion (past or present) can the image of the Goddess be seen more prominently than in Ancient Egypt. Modern history has seen the rise of patriarchy and the supplanting of the images and symbolic teachings of the Goddess. However, these mystical symbols and teachings are not dead but lie dormant and may be discovered and experienced if the keys to mystical wisdom are well understood and if the teachings of mystical wisdom are practiced through rituals and exercises designed to cleanse the heart and promote divine inspiration.

The female principle is prominent in Ancient Egyptian mythology and religious iconography because there was a recognition that Creation is composed of complementary opposites. This means that Creation is a mixture of both male and female elements which cannot exist without each other. The Ancient Egyptian Sages discovered that when there is an imbalance between these principles, there is strife and unrest in human life. When there is balance and harmony, there is peace and prosperity. Therefore, the God must have his female counterpart, the Goddess, and vice versa. This teaching brings up many principles of tantric philosophy. Many of these will be discussed throughout this volume. For more information on this topic see the book *Egyptian Tantra Yoga* from the Egyptian Yoga Book Series by Dr. Muata Ashby.

If you have read any of the books in the Egyptian Yoga series you will already be acquainted with the idea that the origins of Ancient Egypt reach far back into distant antiquity, perhaps as far back as 36,000 B.C.E. or even earlier. You will also be familiar with the idea that the Ancient Egyptians practiced Yoga, not just the exercises, but the mystical philosophy which assists the individual to discover the Higher Self within.

The teachings which are today known as yoga philosophy in India were practiced in ancient times in the Temple of Isis in Ancient Egypt. This volume is divided into four parts. Part one will give you an idea of what the teachings were all about, what was their purpose, and what is the ultimate goal of all spiritual disciplines. Part two will provide a look at the forms of the Goddess and their attributes. In Part Three we will explore the Teachings of the Temple of Isis in more detail. The final section will contain the ceremonies of Ushet Rekhat or Mother Worship.

Religion and Yoga

In its complete form, religion is composed of three aspects, *mythology, ritual* and *metaphysical* or the *mystical experience* (mysticism - mystical philosophy). While many religions contain rituals, traditions, metaphors and myths, there are few professionals trained in the understanding of their deeper aspects and psychological implications (metaphysics and mystical). Thus, there is disappointment, frustration and disillusionment among many followers as well as leaders within many religions, particularly in the Western Hemisphere, because it is difficult to evolve spiritually without the proper spiritual guidance. Through introspection and spiritual research it is possible to discover mythological vistas within religion which can rekindle the light

8

of spirituality, and at the same time increase the possibility of gaining a fuller experience of life. The exoteric (outer, ritualistic) forms of religion with which most people are familiar is only the tip of an iceberg so to speak; it is only a beginning, an invitation or prompting to seek a deeper (esoteric) discovery of the transcendental truths of existence.

Yoga is the practice of mental, physical and spiritual disciplines which lead to self-control and self-discovery by purifying the mind, body and spirit, so as to discover the deeper spiritual essence which lies within every human being and object in the universe. It is this deeper essence which is referred to as God, Goddess, Divine Self, Higher Self, Pure Consciousness, etc. In essence, the goal of yoga practice is to unite or *yoke* one's individual consciousness with universal or cosmic consciousness. Therefore, Ancient Egyptian religious practice, especially in terms of the rituals and other practices of the Ancient Egyptian temple system known as *Shetaut Neter* (the way of the hidden Supreme Being), may be termed as a yoga system: *Egyptian Yoga*. In this sense, religion, in its purest form, is a yoga system, as it seeks to reunite people with their true and original source.

The disciplines of Yoga fall under five major categories, these are *Yoga of Wisdom, Yoga of Devotional Love, Yoga of Meditation, Tantric Yoga* and *Yoga of Selfless Action*. Within these categories there are subsidiary forms which are part of the main disciplines. The emphasis, in the Osirian Myth, *The Ausarian Resurrection*, is on the Yoga of Wisdom, Yoga of Devotional Love and the Yoga of Selfless Action. The important point to remember is that all aspects of yoga can and should be used in an integral fashion to effect an efficient and harmonized spiritual movement in the practitioner. Therefore, while there may be an area of special emphasis, other elements are bound to become part of the yoga program as needed. For example, while a yogin may place emphasis on the yoga of wisdom, they may also practice devotional yoga and meditation yoga along with the wisdom studies.

So the practice of any discipline that leads to oneness with Supreme Consciousness is called yoga. If you study, rationalize and reflect upon the teachings, you are practicing *Yoga of Wisdom*. If you meditate upon the teachings and your Higher Self, you are practicing *Yoga of Meditation*. If you practice rituals which identify you with your spiritual nature, you are practicing *Yoga of Ritual Identification* (which is part of the yoga of wisdom and the yoga of devotional love of the Divine). If you develop your physical nature and psychic energy centers, you are practicing *Serpent Power (Kundalini or Uraeus) Yoga* (which is part of Tantric Yoga). If you practice living according to the teachings of ethical behavior and selflessness, you are practicing *Yoga of Action* (Maat) in daily life. If you practice turning your attention towards the Divine by developing love for the Divine, then it is called *Devotional Yoga* or *Yoga of Divine Love*. The practitioner of yoga is called a yogin (male practitioner) or yogini (female practitioner), and one who has attained the culmination of yoga (union with the Divine) is called a yogi. In this manner, yoga has been developed into many disciplines which may be used in an integral fashion to achieve the same goal: Enlightenment.

PART I: The Myths of The Goddess

In order to begin the journey into the teaching of the goddess we will explore the major Ancient Egyptian myths related to her. First we will explore the myth of Hetheru and Djehuti which extols the glories of the goddess in the form of Hetheru, The Eye of Ra. Then we will see the goddess in her form as Aset in the Myth of Ra and Aset and in the Myth of The Ausarian Resurrection. The mystical teachings contained in each myth will be presented in Part II

The Path of the Goddess

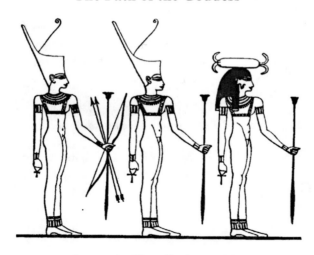

Figure 1: The Goddess Net

Goddess Net

Net is the goddess of creation and war, as well as honor and decisive action. Her attributes are the bow, shield and arrows. She is androgynous (neither male nor female), and was known to watch over Asar's ceremonial bed when he lay dead, along with Aset and Nebthet. She assisted Djehuti in bringing justice for Heru in the Asarian myth. The goddess Net is the primordial Supreme Divinity with female aspect. She is the ancient form of the goddesses Aset and Hetheru, and her worship extended to the far reaches of antiquity, into the Pre-Dynastic period of Ancient Egyptian history. There are records from both priests and priestesses who served the temples of goddess Net. These show that worship of her was most popular, and expressed generally throughout the land of Egypt in ancient times. As we will see, the teachings related to goddess Net are profound and in every way as elevated as those of the Supreme Divinities of Ancient Egypt which portray the male aspect.

In *Pyramid Text* line 606, Net, together with Aset, Nebethet and Serqet, watched over the funerary bed of Asar. The bandages and shrouds used for the mummy of the deceased was given by goddess Net and through these she imparts her protection as well as her blessings in the form of spiritual power.

In *Pyramid Text* line 620-627, it is explained that the initiate is Sebek, the god who is the son of Net, and that the initiate rises like the son of Net. In the city of Net, Sebek is recognized as a form of Heru. Therefore, there is no conflict in finding that the goddess Aset was ascribed her attributes in the later dynastic period. The following speech of the goddess is also used by goddess Aset.

> **"I am everything which has been, and which is, and which shall be and there has never been anyone who has uncovered my veil."**

Of the goddess it is said that she:

> **"Created the seed of the gods and goddesses and men and women."**

Net is the Goddess of Light, and thus her festival is characterized by the practice of lighting candles, torches and lamps. As light she gave birth to Ra, the sun divinity, who lights up the world.

Net is the:

> **"Divine Cow who gave birth to Ra."**

Thus, Net is *Mehurt*, the primeval waters from which creation arose.

Her androgynous nature is related in the following epithet:

> **"Father of all fathers and mother of all mothers."**

> **"Net-Menhit, the Great Lady, Lady of the south, the great cow who gave birth to the sun, who made the seed of the gods and goddesses and men and women, the mother of Ra, the one who raised up Tem in the primeval time,[1] who existed when nothing else had existence and who created that which exists after she came into existence."**

The goddess gave birth to the gods and goddesses and to human beings, but she herself was not given birth. She brought herself into existence and gave birth without being impregnated. She was the primeval ocean and she emerged as herself out of herself and all has come forth through and from her. She is self-existent, and her nature is secret, a mystery to all.

shetat - deep mysterious nature of the goddess Net

---

[1] At the time of Creation.

Net is also referred to as:

"Ua-netert"
"Divinity One"

Thus, Net encompasses the non-dual, absolute, all-encompassing divinity, i.e., she is Neberdjer. This teaching is further illustrated through the hieroglyphic symbols of her name.

Her symbols are the bow, ⌣⌣⌣, two arrows, ←₩, the shield, ⋈, and the knitting spool, ⛧ .

The name *Net*, ⌒ ⛧, is a play on the word *nt*, ⌒ ,or *ntet*, ⌒⌒, meaning that which is, that which exists, i.e. that which is real, true, and abiding. The goddess provides *saa*, ⫯⫯⫯, or protection for the spiritual aspirant. She uses a bow and arrow to shoot down the enemies of the righteous (anger, hatred, greed, jealousy, envy, lust, etc.).

In her name of *Net hetep*, ✕⌣, the goddess is the abiding supreme peace.

Net is also known as Amentet, the hidden goddess and consort of the god Amen as well as Rat, the consort of the god Ra. Thus we are to understand that all the goddess forms are in reality aspects of Net.

Net is also known as *Mehenit*, ∿⫯⫯⌒⛧, the weaving goddess. The material woven by the goddess is used for wrapping the mummy, but she also weaves her own clothing. This clothing is the outer appearance of the physical universe. The objective of spiritual movement within the *het Net*, ⎕⌒⛧⊗, the house of Net (Creation), is to propitiate the goddess to remove her clothing, to unveil herself, so that the initiate may see her true form...absolute existence.

Mysticism of the Ancient Egyptian Goddess

Being the Goddess of Light and having the power to weave the intricate web of Creation wherein all is connected, the goddess allows herself to be disrobed by those who follow the path to her discovery. This path was given in the Temple of Aset, who is a later form of goddess Net. In the temple of Aset the path of spirituality (Shetaut Aset), known today as the Yoga of Wisdom, was taught. It is a spiritual discipline involving the following areas. The aspirant is to purify of the body through a vegetarian diet, control of the sex urge, engage in devotional practices and study of the wisdom teachings.[2] **Stage 1: Listening** to the teachings of the myth of the goddess and receiving mystical insights into these.[3] **Stage 2: Reflecting** on those teachings, and living life in accordance with virtue and truth (i.e. practice of the teachings in daily life). **Stage 3: Through Subtle One-pointed Mentation,** leading oneself to a meditative union with the Goddess who is the essence of light, which transcends mind, body, time and space.

How to Follow the Path of the Goddess Net

For those wishing more details on the path of Goddess Net and Aset, there are special materials that have been prepared to augment the teaching presented here as well as the practice of studying and living the mystic path of the goddess. These are: The book *The Wisdom of Isis*, the audio lecture *The Festival of Lights: Worship of Goddess Net*, the Audio Music and Chanting CD or Cassette *Glories of the Divine Mother*. Contact the Sema Institute for more information (305) 378-6253.

---

[2] Chanting, singing, prayer.
[3] See the book *The Wisdom of Isis* by Muata Ashby.

The Story of Hetheru and Djehuti

This is the story of Hetheru (Hathor) and Djehuti (Djehuti) which was written in Ancient Egypt thousands of years ago. It was told on temple inscriptions. Hetheru is the goddess of beauty and passion. She has many forms. At times she is a beautiful woman, at others she is a cow, and still at others she is the Eye of Ra, the very scorching power of the sun itself.

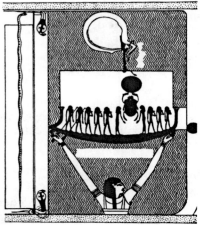

THE CREATION

Ra is the Creator of the universe. He is the very source of all that exists. The *Pautti* or *Psedjet* (Ennead or nine divinities), the primordial gods and goddesses of Creation, emanated from the Supreme Being. Ra or Ra-Tem arose out of the *"Nu,"* the Primeval waters, the hidden essence, and began sailing the *"Boat of Millions of Years"* which included the "neteru." The neteru of the Pautti are Ra-Atum, Shu, Tefnut, Geb, Nut, Osiris, Isis, Set, and Nephthys. Hathor, Djehuti and Maat came into existence at the instant of Creation.

One day Hetheru left Egypt and traveled south into the land of Nubia. She transformed herself into the form of a lioness or lynx. When she left Egypt it was devastated. Gloom filled the atmosphere. Everything was in decline. The forces of darkness, chaos, injustice, unrighteousness and evil began to take control of the land because Hetheru, who was the power of Ra which he used to uphold righteousness and truth, had left the land. Ra, the Supreme Being, creator of the gods and goddesses and the entire universe, became sorrowful at the loss of his daughter, his very power. Hetheru took pleasure in her new form. She killed everything she could find. She lived in the forest and took delight in causing fear and pain. Ra called the gods and goddesses and asked who would bring his beautiful daughter back.

Everyone was afraid because as the Eye of Ra, Hetheru held the power of life and death over all things. In her new form Hetheru lived the life of a predator. She hunted

15

and killed anything that came into her view without discrimination or remorse. So Ra called the god Djehuti and asked him to find and bring back the beautiful Hetheru. Djehuti realized that if he was to accomplish this dangerous task he would need to be clever in order to avoid being Hetheru's next meal.

Djehuti transformed himself into the form of a harmless baboon and then he set out to find Hetheru. He found Hetheru sitting alone, licking her paws. He crept closer to her and made noise to announce his approach. When Hetheru realized that something was approaching she immediately took an offensive stance and prepared to fight. Then Djehuti called out, "Hail O beautiful daughter of the Sun!" As soon as Hetheru noticed that it was only a baboon she took poise and immediately Djehuti asked if he could speak with her.

THE FIRST PARABLE

Hetheru replied, "Say what you have to say and then I will eat you." Then Djehuti replied, "You certainly have the power to kill me, but you should think about the parable of the vulture and the wildcat."

Hetheru instructed him, "What is this parable? Tell me right now," and then she sat down. Djehuti began to speak immediately so as to keep her attention captivated with interest, "There was a mother vulture and a mother wildcat who were close neighbors. The vulture had four chicks and the wildcat had given birth to four kittens. The mother vulture and the mother wildcat had a big problem. Their children were hungry but the two mothers were both afraid to leave them alone because they feared that either one of them would kill the other's children for food.

The mothers arranged a truce between them by swearing an oath upon the name of Ra. They swore that neither one would hurt the other's children. So now they both felt secure enough to go out and start hunting food for their children. For some time the truce worked and soon the vulture chicks and the kittens began to grow.

One day, one of the vulture chicks went to the area where the kittens were playing. He snatched away a portion of their food. One of the kittens reached out and swatted the chick, injuring it, and told it to find its own food. The chick could not fly but had enough strength to tell the kitten, "you have broken the oath between our families and Ra will punish you for this great injustice."

When the mother vulture returned she noticed that her chick was lying on the ground so she figured that the wildcat had broken her promise. The next time that the wildcat left to go hunting the mother vulture killed all of the kittens and brought them back to her nest for food.

When the mother wildcat returned she realized that the mother vulture had killed her kittens, so she cried out to Ra, "O Divine one who upholds justice and righteousness, punish the evil doer who has broken the oath which was sworn upon your name!" Ra heard this plea and set the plan in motion to carry out the punishment for this transgression.

The next day as the mother vulture was hunting she came upon a campfire which had a portion of meat being cooked and there was no one in sight. She swooped down and grabbed it and quickly returned to her nest and dropped it there for her chicks to feast on. She had not noticed that there was a smoldering piece of coal attached to the meat. The nest caught fire and the three chicks were burnt to death. Noticing this the mother wildcat yelled out, "You killed my children and now Ra has punished you!"

Djehuti explained, "Oh Glorious Lady (Hetheru) do you see the omniscience and justice of Ra, who sees and hears all things? He is the giver of life and all of nature owes its existence to him. He controls every particle of Creation. He is the sustainer of Creation. His justice is perfect. Praises be to him and praises be to you who are his daughter!"

Hetheru began to reflect upon the meaning of this parable and she began to remember her father and the wonderful relationship they shared in the past.

Djehuti took advantage of the opportunity and moved closer to her and said, "Oh Divine Lady, I bring you an offering of divine food from the abode of the Sun god (Ra). It brings health and joy to all who eat it."

Hetheru began to relax and saw no harm in accepting the tribute from the humble baboon.

THE WISDOM OF THE ORIGINS CREATION

As the beautiful goddess consumed the offering Djehuti began to speak again, "These herbs come from the land of Egypt. Egypt is the land which rose up from the Nun, the Primeval Waters, in ancient times. It was created for the gods and goddesses. It is also the home of your Divine Father and your brother Shu. All beings long to return to the land of their birth. Who can be happy living away from the very source of happiness where they were born?"

Hetheru had forgotten her true identity and had become addicted to the taste of blood. Now she began to remember the wonder of her Divine Father, Egypt and her own true identity. She began to think about her temples in Egypt and how men and women had brought her offerings and revered her beauty as the most exalted of all goddesses. Hetheru was so overwhelmed by these memories and feelings that she began to cry.

Djehuti spoke again, "Oh Great Lady, you are crying now but think of the pain of the people in Egypt who are deprived of your glories. Due to your absence there is no merriment, no singing, no parties in Egypt, and the evil doers are going unpunished. Return with me and I will tell you more stories of Egypt."

As soon as she heard this Hetheru realized that he was trying to get her to go back to Egypt and she became exceedingly angry. She growled and made terrible sounds and Djehuti immediately prostrated himself and begged for mercy in the name of Ra, "Oh Divine Lady, before you kill me listen to this important parable about the two vultures."

THE SECOND PARABLE

Hetheru calmed down because she was intrigued by the words of Djehuti. He quickly began to speak. "Once upon a time there were two vultures in the forest. One said to the other, "My eyes are so perfect that I can see all things to the end of the earth." The other vulture said, "Well I can hear everything. I can even hear Ra as he decrees the fate of all Creation."

The two vultures debated about which gift is better. The vulture with the keen hearing said, "Another bird far away told him that an fly was eaten by a lizard. The lizard was then eaten by a snake and then the snake was caught by a hawk. The snake was so heavy that the snake and the hawk fell into the sea. Can you tell me what is happening now by looking with your keen eyesight?"

The vulture with the keen eyesight replied, "The hawk and the snake have been swallowed by a fish and that fish was swallowed up by a larger fish. The bigger fish came to close to shore and a lion grabbed it out of the sea. Then a legendary creature called *Sefer* (Sfr) or griffin (English) flew to the area and carried off the lion.

One vulture said to the other, "This remarkable scene that we have witnessed proves the power of Ra. Even the existence of the fly was noticed, and the consequence of killing will be punished by one's own death. But how is it that the Sefer has survived all of this?" The other vulture answered, "It must be that the Sefer is the messenger of Ra who was sent out to carry out the law of Ra. The Sefer is the most powerful of all creatures."

So Djehuti began to explain the moral of the parable, "Oh Great Lady, do you see how the Divine Father rewards goodness with goodness and evil with evil? In this manner the balance of the universe is maintained by the Great God. Oh Great Lady, you have been endowed with Ra's power. You are the Eye of Ra. You have the power to carry out the law of Ra. You are the most powerful force in all of Creation."

After hearing this the goddess' eyes filled with joy and she began to feel pride in being the daughter of Ra. She told Djehuti, "You may now relax, humble one, I no longer desire to kill and eat you. Your words have captivated me and I know that you are a beneficent being."

They began to walk towards Egypt and Djehuti began to recite another parable.

THE THIRD PARABLE

Djehuti began, "Once upon a time there were two jackals who were great friends. One day, as they rested, suddenly they saw a lion running towards them. Much to the lion's surprise they did not attempt to run away. When the lion reached them it stopped and asked them why they did not try to run away. The jackals replied that the lion would catch them anyway so there was no point in running away and getting tired in a futile effort to escape. The lion was so pleased with their calm and truthful answer that he spared their life.

Djehuti said to Hetheru, "Let us walk towards Egypt and I will protect you on the way." Hetheru raised her eyebrow at him as soon as she heard this and replied, "How can you protect me? The Eye of the Sun is the most powerful force and it needs no protection, especially from a baboon!"

Djehuti replied, "The strong sometimes need help from those who are weaker. Do you recall the parable of the mouse and the lion? I will tell you."

THE FOURTH PARABLE

Djehuti began to tell the parable as they walked towards Egypt. "There was a lion who lived as a king. He was so powerful that all the other animals feared him. One day the lion came upon a panther who was badly wounded. The lion asked the panther who had injured him and the panther told him that man was responsible for his injuries. The lion never heard of an animal called man. He decided to hunt man. On the way to find man the lion met a mule, an ox, a cow, a bear and another lion. All of them had been outsmarted by man even though they were more powerful than man. They all said that man was the most cunning creature even though he appeared to be feeble and weak. They told the powerful lion to stay away from man. This only made the lion more determined to find man.

On the way the lion came across a small mouse. Without a thought the lion raised a paw to crush the mouse but the mouse pleaded for mercy and pledged to be the lion's friend in his time of need. The lion asked him, "How can you ever help me? I am more powerful than any creature." The mouse replied, "Do not be so sure of yourself. Sometimes the weak can help the powerful." The lion let him go and went on his way. Soon after the encounter with the mouse the lion fell into a pit and was tangled up in a net so strongly that he could not escape. The lion expected to die the next day when man would find him. The lion heard a screeching little voice. It was the little mouse. The mouse worked upon the ropes all night, and before man could come to check the net, the lion had been freed from the death trap. So Great Lady," Djehuti began, "every power will someday meet a higher power and the weak can sometimes help those who are strong."

SFR
(Griffin)

CONCLUSION

As they entered Egypt the goddess was met with praises from the people who were rejoicing at her return. Before entering the city of Waset (Thebes), Hetheru laid down to rest. She fell asleep and the watchful eye of Djehuti looked after her as she withdrew into the land of slumber.

The enemies of Ra were not pleased with her return so they plotted against her. In the middle of the night they sent a serpent of chaos to poison her in order to leave Ra defenseless, deprived of his protecting Eye. However, Djehuti, who was vigilant all of the time, noticed the serpent and woke Hetheru. Still in the form of a wildcat, Hetheru leaped on the serpent and broke the serpent's back. She was grateful to Djehuti and recalled the wonderful parable of the mouse and the lion. She knew now that everything that Djehuti had said was true.

In the city of Waset there was a great feast in her honor which lasted for seven days. Hetheru was so gratified that she transformed into the form of a beautiful, soothing, gentle and kind woman. Then she and Djehuti continued to move Northward. They reached the sacred city of Anu (Heliopolios), the home of Ra. Also, there was rejoicing in the city of Het-ku-Ptah. When Hetheru and Ra held each other once again all of the gods and goddesses rejoiced. Djehuti transformed himself back into his original form and then Hetheru recognized him and her heart looked on him with love and gratitude.

Dua Hetheru!
Dua Hetheru!
Dua Hetheru!
Dua Hetheru!

The Myth of Asar, Aset and Heru

Introduction

We have seen how the Divine Self in the form of Ra created the world and all living creatures. Also we have seen how the goddess in the form of Hetheru was called upon by Ra to punish unrighteous people. Ra later decided that there should be a divine incarnation of himself. The teaching about the divine incarnation exists in all parts of the world. Some examples of it are Jesus, Krishna, Buddha and others. Ra decreed that the world needed someone to lead it, to teach it the proper way to live, the way which leads to blessedness and spiritual enlightenment. For this purpose Asar (Osiris) and Aset (Isis) who had come into existence when Ra emerged from the Primeval Ocean and Creation came into being now came into the world and assumed the rulership of Egypt and brought civilization to the world. Here begins the Story of Asar, Aset and Heru.

Asar and Aset dedicated themselves to the welfare of humanity and sought to spread civilization throughout the earth, even as far as India and China.

The goddess Aset sought for higher wisdom and power in order to rule over the world in a better way and also to help her son Heru face his struggles and challenges in life. She began to meditate on this noble desire. This was the beginning of the first story within the myth of Asar, Aset and Heru...

Dua Asar, Aset, Heru!
Dua Asar, Aset, Heru!
Dua Asar, Aset, Heru!
Dua Asar, Aset, Heru!

THE STORY OF RA AND ASET

This is the story of Ra and Aset. Ra is the Supreme Divinity. Ra is the source of all Creation. Ra is the essence of all life, fire, the gods and goddesses, men and women, beasts, cattle, reptiles, birds, fish and all objects in Creation. Ra's names and forms are innumerable and un-knowable even by the gods and goddesses. Ra is so ancient that periods of one hundred and twenty-five years for human beings are like periods of a year for him.

Behold the goddess Aset. She was living in the form of a woman in ancient times. She was knowledgeable in the words of power and the wisdom of the world. Aset had no desire for human existence. She was dispassionate towards human beings. She revered the state of the gods and goddesses and revered even more, the state of the spirits, because they were closer to the Divine.

21

Mysticism of the Ancient Egyptian Goddess

Aset meditated in her heart as follows, "Is it possible for me to become like Ra and to be the supreme monarch of all Creation by knowing the name of Ra?"

One day as Ra made his entrance in the eastern horizon, a portion of his essence fell upon the earth. Aset took this and mixed it with earth and fashioned it into the form of a serpent.

She left the serpent on the road which the great god traveled. The serpent bit Ra and caused him to become ill. He became so ill that the gods and goddesses feared he would die. Nobody could find an antidote to the serpent's bite.

Then Aset came along to speak to her father Ra and said: "What is this, Oh Divine Father? What is it? Hath a serpent shot his venom into thee? Hath a thing which thou has fashioned lifted up its head against thee? Verily it shall be overthrown by beneficent words of power, and I will make it to retreat in the sight of thy rays." The holy god opened his month and said, "I was walking along the road and passing through the two lands which I myself had created, the two lands of my country, when I was bitten by a serpent which I did not see. I am colder than water, I am hotter than fire, all my members sweat, I myself quake, mine eye is unsteady. I cannot look at the heavens, and water forces itself on my face as in the time of the inundation."

And Aset said to Ra, "Oh my Divine Father, tell me thy name, for whoever is able to pronounce his name liveth." Ra replied, "I am the maker of the heavens and the earth, I have knit together the mountains, and I have created everything which exist upon them. I am the maker of the waters (Primeval Ocean), and I have made Meht-ur to come into being; I have made the Bull of his Mother, and I have made the joys of love (love-making) to exist. I am the maker of heaven, and I have made to be hidden the two gods of the horizon, and I have placed the souls of the gods and goddesses within them. I am the being who opens his eyes and the light comes forth; I am the being who shuts his eyes and there is darkness. I am the being who gives the command, and the waters of Hapi (the Nile) burst forth. I am the being whose name the gods and goddesses know not. I am the maker of the hours and the creator of the days. I am the opener (i.e., inaugurator) of the festivals, and the maker of the floods of water. I am the creator of the fire of life whereby the works of the houses are caused to come into being. I am Kheper in the morning, Ra at the time of culmination (i.e., noon), and Temu in the evening."

Goddess Worship and Rituals of Enlightenment

Aset and Ra

Even though Ra said these great and wonderful things the poison was not driven from its course, and the great god felt no improvement in his condition. Then Aset said to Ra, "Among the things which you have said to me thy name has not been mentioned. Oh declare it unto me and the poison shall come forth for the person who hath declared his name shall live." Then Ra said, "I will allow myself to be searched through by Aset, and my name shall come forth from my body and go into hers." Then the divine one hid himself from the gods and goddesses, and the throne in the Boat of Millions of Years was empty. And it came to pass that when it was the time for the heart to come forth [from the god], she said unto her son Heru: "The great god is bound by an oath to give his two eyes." Thus, the great god yielded up his name, and Aset, the Great Lady of enchantments, said, "Flow on, poison, and come forth from Ra; let the Eye of Horus come forth from the god and illumine all things outside of his mouth. I have worked, and I make the poison to fall on the ground, for the venom has been mastered. Verily the name hath been taken away from the great god. Let Ra live, and let the poison die; and if the poison live then Ra shall die. And similarly, a certain man, the son of a certain man, shall live and the poison shall die." These were the words which spoke Aset, the Great Lady, the mistress of the gods, and she had knowledge of Ra in his own name. The above words shall be said over an image of Temu, Heru-Hekennuu, Aset or Heru.

Aset continued to rule over Egypt while Asar was traveling around the world. During the absence of Asar from his kingdom, his brother Set had no opportunity to make innovations in the state, because Aset was extremely vigilant in governing the country, and always upon her guard and watchful for any irregularity or unrighteousness.

Asar

Upon Asar's return from touring the world and carrying the teachings of wisdom abroad, there was merriment and rejoicing throughout the land. However, one day after Asar's return, through his lack of vigilance he became intoxicated and slept with Set's wife, Nebthet. Nebthet loved Asar and seized the opportunity to sleep with Asar at a time when he was not vigilant, since she looks just like Aset, except for her headdress. Nebthet, as a result of the union with Asar, begot Anpu.

Set, who represents the personification of evil forces, plotted in jealousy and anger (the blinding passion that prevents forgiveness and understanding) to usurp the throne and conspired to kill Asar. Set secretly got the measurements of Asar and constructed a coffin. Through trickery, Set was able to get Asar to "try on" the coffin for size. While Asar was resting in the coffin, Set and his assistants locked it and then dumped it into the Nile river.

The coffin made its way to the coast of Syria where it became embedded in the earth and from it grew a tree with the most pleasant aroma in the form of a Djed or Tet. The Tet is the symbol of Asar's back. It has four horizontal lines in relation to a firmly established, straight column. The Djed column is symbolic of the upper energy centers (chakras) that relate to the levels of consciousness of the spirit.

Aset receiving the Djed Pillar from the Syrian King

The King of Syria was out walking and as he passed by the tree, he immediately fell in love with the pleasant aroma, so he had the tree cut down and brought to his palace. Aset, Asar's wife, who is the personification of the life giving, mother force in Creation and in all humans, went to Syria in search of Asar. Her search led her to the palace of the Syrian King where she took a job as the nurse of the King's son. Every evening Aset would put the boy into the "fire" to consume his mortal parts, thereby transforming him to immortality. Fire is symbolic of both physical and mental purification. Most importantly, fire implies wisdom, the light of truth, illumination and energy which burns away ignorance and egoism. Aset, by virtue of her qualities, has the power to bestow immortality through the transformative power of her symbolic essence. She symbolizes intuitional wisdom which leads to the eradication of mortal consciousness and the birth of immortal continuousness. Aset then told the king that Asar, her husband, was inside the pillar he made from the tree. He graciously gave her the pillar (Djed) and she returned with it to Kamit (Kmt, Egypt). With the assistance of the crocodile god Sebek, Aset brought the body of Asar back to Kemet.

Above: The Birth of Heru

Mysticism of the Ancient Egyptian Goddess

(Aset asisted by Djehuti and Amun)

Below: The goddess Serket

Upon her return to Kmt, Aset went to the papyrus swamps where she lay over Asar's dead body and fanned him with her wings, infusing him with new life. In this manner Aset revived Asar through her power of love and wisdom, and then they united once more. From their union was conceived a son, Heru (Horus), with the assistance of the gods Djehuti (Tehuti) and Amon. Heru, therefore, was born from the union of the spirit of Asar and the life giving power of Aset (physical nature). Thus, Heru represents the union of spirit and matter, and the renewed life of Asar, his rebirth.

One evening, as Set was hunting in the papyrus swamps, he came upon Aset and Asar. In a rage of passion he dismembered the body of Asar into several pieces and scattered the pieces throughout the land. In this way, it is Set, the brute force of our bodily impulses and lower desires that "dismembers" our higher intellect. Instead of oneness and unity, we see multiplicity and separateness which give rise to egoistic (selfish) and violent behavior. The Great Mother, Aset, once again set out to search, now for the pieces of Asar, with the help of Anpu and Nebthet.

After searching all over the world, they found all the pieces of Asar's body, except for his phallus which was eaten by a fish. In Eastern Hindu-Tantra mythology, the God Shiva, who is the equivalent of Asar, also lost his phallus in one story. In Ancient Egyptian and Hindu-Tantra mythology, this loss represents seminal retention and celibacy in order to channel the sexual energy to the higher spiritual centers, thereby transforming it into spiritual energy. Aset, through her love, devotion and wisdom, and with the help of Apuat and Nebthet re-membered the pieces of Asar, all except the phallus which was eaten by a fish. Asar thus regained life and became king of the realm of the dead.

Aset took Heru into hiding so that he could grow up safely away from Set. One day Set sent an evil scorpion to find Heru and kill him so that he could not grow up to challenge him for the throne of Kemet. The scorpion found Heru and stung and killed him. When Aset found out about this she was so grief stricken that her cry was heard to the farthest reaches of the universe. When Ra, the Supreme Being, heard it, he stopped his movement. This effectively brought the entire universe to a standstill. In response to Aset, Ra sent Djehuti to assist Aset. Djehuti carried special words of power which allowed him to revive Heru.

When Heru became a young man, Asar returned from the realm of the dead and encouraged him to take up arms (vitality, wisdom, courage, strength of will) and establish truth, justice and righteousness in the world by challenging Set, its current ruler.

The scorpion goddess Selket assisted Aset in her time of sorrow over the death of Heru and Asar. She comforted Aset in her time of grief. She acted as the voice of reason, suggesting that Aset should call out to the Barque of Ra for assistance when Heru was killed. This episode attests to the understanding that even though Selket is a scorpion, like the one which killed Heru, her power to cause injury was turned to a positive end. So the same mental energy, as symbolized by the scorpion, can be used to promote negativity by associating with the ego (Set) or positive spiritual movement when aligned with wisdom (Aset).

The Battle of Heru (Heru) and Set

The battle between Heru and Set took many twists, sometimes one seeming to get the upper hand and sometimes the other, yet neither one gaining a clear advantage in order to decisively win. At one point, Aset tried to help Heru by catching Set, but due to the pity and compassion she felt towards him, she set him free. In a passionate rage, Heru cut off her head and went off by himself in a frustrated state. Even Heru is susceptible to passion which leads to performing deeds that one later regrets. Set found Heru and gouged out Heru's eyes. During this time, Heru was overpowered by the evil of Set. He became blinded to truth (as signified by the loss of his eyes) and thus, was unable to do battle (act with Maat) with Set . His power of sight was later restored by Hetheru and Djehuti. Hetheru is the Goddess of passionate love, desire and fierce power, who also represents the left Eye of Ra. She is the fire spitting, destructive power of light, which dispels the darkness (blindness) of ignorance. Djehuti represents knowledge and right reasoning, the power of the mind to see spiritual truth. He brings subtlety of intellect to understand the deeper meaning of the teachings.

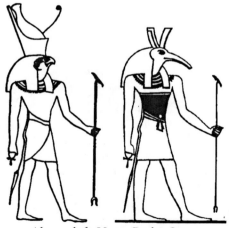

Above: left- Heru. Right- Set

When the conflict resumed, the two contendants went before the court of the Psedjet divinities (company of the nine gods who ruled over Creation, headed by Ra). Set, promising to end the fight and restore Heru to the throne, invited Heru to spend the night at his house, but Heru soon found out that Set had evil intentions when he tried to have intercourse with him. The uncontrolled Set also symbolizes unrestricted sexual activity. Therefore, all sexual desires should be pursued in accordance with moral and intellectual principles which dictate rules of propriety that lead to health, and personal, societal and spiritual order (Maat). Juxtaposed against this aspect of Set (uncontrolled sexual potency and desire) is Heru in the form of ithyphallic (erect phallus) Min, who represents not only the control of sexual desire, but its sublimation as well (see Min and Hetheru). Min symbolizes the power which comes from the sublimation of the sexual energy.

Through more treachery and deceit, Set attempted to destroy Heru with the help of the Psedjet, by tricking them into believing that Heru was not worthy of the throne. Asar sent a letter pleading with the Psedjet to do what is correct. Heru, as the son of Asar, should be the rightful heir to the throne. All but two of them (the Psedjet) agreed because Heru, they said, was too young to rule. Asar then sent them a second letter (scroll of papyrus with a message) reminding them that even they cannot escape judgment for their deeds; they will be judged in the end when they have to finally go to the West (abode of the dead).

This signifies that even the gods and goddesses cannot escape judgment for their deeds and that their existence is finite. Since all that exists is only a manifestation of the absolute reality which goes beyond time and space, that which is in the realm of time and space (humans, spirits, gods, angels, neteru) are all bound by its laws.

Following the receipt of Asar's scroll (letter), Heru was crowned King of Egypt. Set accepted the decision and made peace with Heru. All the gods and goddesses rejoiced. Thus ends the legend of Asar, Aset, and Heru.

Dua Aset!
Dua Aset!
Dua Aset!
Dua Aset!

PART II: The Mystical Teachings Of The Myths of the Goddess

The teachings of the goddess appear in two ways. The myths themselves provide the essential mystical wisdom necessary to promote spiritual evolution if they are correctly interpreted. The myths were presented in Part I. This section will present the mystical teachings contained in those myths and the Yogic philosophy which underlies the image, symbols and events which the goddess represents.

Secondly, the teachings and practices of the Temple of Aset are perhaps best known because the worship of Aset (Isis), having originated in pre-dynastic times (before 3,000 B.C.E.), remained very strong even during the early Christian era and during the reign of the Roman Empire, up to the time of its demise (c. 450-550 A.C.E.). At around 200 to 100 B.C.E. the most important Temple of Isis of the Roman Empire was in "Campus Martius." The Campus Martius was located on the Tiber River near ancient Rome. The teachings of the Temple of Aset will be summarized following the glosses on the myths of the Goddess.

A GLOSS ON THE STORY OF HETHOR AND DJEHUTI

The Goddess Hetheru

In a text from the Temple at Dier al-Medina, Hetheru is referred to as having the same divine attributes as Horus. She is described as *"The Golden One"* and *"The Queen of the Gods."* Her shrines being even more numerous than those of Horus, Hathor or *Het-Heru*, meaning *"The House of Horus"* and *"The House Above* (sky),*"* became identified, like Horus, with the salvation of the initiate. In the *Egyptian Book of Coming Forth By Day*, she is the one who urges the initiate to do battle with the monster Apep so as not to lose his / her heart as she cries out: *"Take your armor."* In a separate papyrus, the initiate is told that she (Hetheru) is the one who *will make your face perfect among the Gods; she will open your eye so that you may see every day... she will make your legs able to walk with ease in the Underworld. Her name is Hathor, Lady of Amenta.*

Hetheru represents the power of Ra, the Supreme Spirit, therefore, associating with her implies coming into contact with the boundless source of energy which sustains the universe. Making contact with Hathor implies the development of inner will-power which engenders clarity of vision to discern what is righteous from what is unrighteous. A mind which is constantly distracted and beset with fetters (anger, hatred, greed, conceit, covetousness, lust, selfishness, etc.) cannot discern the optimal course in life. It becomes weak willed because the negative emotions and feelings drain the mental energy, thus unrighteous actions and sinful thoughts arise and the weak mind cannot resist them. Unrighteous actions lead to adverse situations and adverse situations lead to pain and sorrow in life. (See *The Ausarian Resurrection* and *Egyptian Tantra Yoga* for more on Hathor and the teachings of Egyptian Tantra Yoga.)

In mystical philosophy, the eyes are understood to be the seat of waking consciousness. When you wake someone you look at their eyes to see if they are awake. The right Eye in particular is seen as the dynamic aspect of consciousness. Hathor, as the right Eye of Ra, symbolizes exactly that concept. God (Ra) has projected consciousness (the Eye) into Creation, and in so doing, the Eye (waking consciousness) becomes involved in various activities within the world of time and space. Similarly, the human soul has projected its image into time and space (the ocean of Creation), and in so doing, the psycho-physical self has emerged and human experience is possible. From this process arises the possibility of karmic involvement as well as ignorance and egoism.

Hetheru as a Metaphor

Hetheru represents the predicament of human life. From a state of unity with the Divine (Ra) she becomes degraded to the point of forgetting her true identity. She engages in violent acts and lives out of the lower nature and base desires. This is known as the state of *Dullness of Mind.* The more a person separates from their essential nature, the more a person slides downward into egoism and the lower aspects of the mind which include vices such as anger, hatred, greed, lust, jealousy, etc. Oftentimes these feelings are so strong that they cloud the intellect and render a person incapable of higher forms of thought or feeling. In her aspect as "The Eye of Ra" Hetheru is the highest power. She is the object of awe and admiration for all. But when her mind was degraded, the same awesome power becomes the object of tremendous fear because it is uncontrolled and destructive.

Once again, all human beings have the power to act with great goodness or extremely evil intent. If a person acts out of Maat (virtues such as compassion, non-violence, truth, universal love, harmony, sharing, etc.) then their capacity for goodness is boundless. However, if a person acts out of vices (listed above), then their capacity for negativity is immense even to the extent of self-destruction. When negativity becomes so intense in the mind, the power of thinking is not the only aspect that becomes impaired. A person's memory and identity becomes impaired as well. Instead of seeing herself as the beautiful goddess of light and the enforcer of truth and justice, Hetheru saw herself as the vicious wildcat of death. In the same manner people have forgotten their identity as gods and goddesses and have come to regard themselves as miserable human beings caught in the struggle of life for survival, in competition with other human beings and with nature itself.

Djehuti took on the task of saving Hetheru from the pit of negativity and ignorance into which she had fallen. Djehuti, a symbol of the Spiritual Preceptor, represents the intellect, right thinking and truth.

Seba Djehuti

Djehuti is the god of learning, writing, mathematics and language. Djehuti is referred to as Thoth by the Greeks. In Ancient Egyptian mythology, he is the scribe of the gods. He appears as the record keeper of the dead in the *Books of Coming Forth By Day.* He is the patron of learning and of the arts. He is the inventor of writing, and in the specific theology related to him, he is also seen as the Creator of the universe. Djehuti is depicted as a man with the head of a baboon or an ibis bird. He also bears pen and ink, and sometimes also the lunar disk and crescent.

The ibis is a wading bird related to the stork and the heron. The choice of the ibis indicates a unique feature or quality which spiritual learning requires. This quality is related to the *wading* nature of the ibis. Wading means *walking in or through a substance, as water, that offers resistance, impedes or makes movement difficult.* Djehuti represents intellect, the mind and its capacity to cut (wade) through the myriad of thoughts and concepts (water-ocean of consciousness) in order to get to the truth.

)

The crescent moon symbol of Djehuti is a figure of the moon in its first quarter. It has concave* and convex** edges terminating in points. The crescent moon symbol signifies growing or increasing understanding, reason and spiritual wisdom. Therefore, Djehuti is the embodiment of knowledge. This is one of the reasons why he is said to have created writing. He is also the messenger of Ra who brings the special words of power to Aset in the Ausarian Resurrection Story in order for Aset to resurrect Heru. In this aspect the symbolizes the Spiritual Preceptor who brings the wisdom of the Divine Self to the aspirant so the aspirant can resurrect his\her spiritual aspiration. (*Curved like the inner surface of a sphere. **Curved outward, as the exterior of a sphere.)

The universe is understood to be like an ocean of matter through which Ra sails on his barque in order to sustain Creation. Djehuti is Ra's mind, the cosmic mind, with which Ra moves through the ocean of Creation. Thus, the universe is known as an ocean of consciousness called Nu or Nun. The spirit (Ra) uses the Cosmic Mind (Djehuti) to create the objects and varied forms of Creation and maintain order in Creation. Therefore, matter (Creation) is in reality consciousness (Primeval Ocean) which has taken on forms (physical objects) in accordance with the will of the Cosmic Mind. The Cosmic Mind also brings forth learning and knowledge to Creation through the arts, sciences and language. Nothing is invented by human beings. Everything that is created by civilization comes from the Cosmic Mind, and not from any individual human being. To believe otherwise would be egoistic thought. The more a person is in tune with the Cosmic Mind the more knowledge he or she can obtain and the more inner peace and fulfillment a person can experience. The farther away a person gets from the Cosmic mind through negative actions, ignorance and delusion, the less able a person is to discover goodness, inner peace, knowledge, happiness and health in life.

Eye of Djehuti

So Djehuti devises a plan to approach Hetheru. Understanding that she is in a state of intense *dullness,* he knows that he cannot approach her directly by using his ordinary form and by giving her direct teachings as to the nature of the Self (Ra) and her true identity (Hetheru, the Eye of Ra). So he decides to transform himself into the form of a humble, harmless looking baboon instead of presenting himself in the form of a regal ibis headed divinity. It would be very difficult for an ordinary person to behold and accept the real form of the Divine Self (Supreme Being). Therefore, the indirect means of religion, yoga, symbols, myth and parables are adopted until a spiritual aspirant is ready to have a direct experience. At that time the indirect means are placed aside in order to experience the Divine who transcends all forms, concepts, religions and symbols. So Djehuti decided to present to Hetheru some of the most profound teachings related to the nature of the Self in the form of parables in order to gradually gain her confidence and stimulate her latent memories of her own true glory.

In the beginning, the Spiritual Preceptor must help the individual to somehow turn the anguish and pain experienced as a result of interaction with the world into a desire to rise above it. To this end, a series of techniques and disciplines have been developed over thousands of years. Some of these methods are myths, parables, mental disciplines, meditation and physical culture (Yoga exercises and development of the internal Life Force). The teacher needs to help the seeker to restructure and channel those energies which arise from disappointment and frustration into a healthy dispassion for the illusoriness of the world and its entanglements. The teacher shows the way to develop spiritual aspiration and self-effort directed at sustaining a viable personal spiritual program or *Sheti*.

Djehuti is the quintessential image of the Guru in this story. The word "Guru" is an Indian Sanskrit term meaning "Spiritual Preceptor," a teacher of spiritual truths. A Spiritual Preceptor is a Sage who shows others the way to understand the higher reality beyond the ordinary phenomenal universe. He or she shows others how to discover their true identity and realize their oneness with the Divine. In essence, they are spiritual guides.

In Ancient Egyptian Mythology there are two great Spiritual Preceptors. Djehuti is one of them. He is the wonderful teacher of Hetheru. The other one is Aset. In the Shetaut Asar or The Story of Asar, Aset and Heru otherwise known as the Ausarian Resurrection, she is the teacher to her son Heru. She trains him in the arts, sciences and the mystical philosophy of Creation and the nature of the Divine Self. She enables Heru to receive the Divine Vision which she obtained from Ra in the Story of Ra and Aset.

The word *Seba* is the Ancient Egyptian term meaning "Spiritual Preceptor" or "Spiritual Counselor or Teacher." A Spiritual Preceptor is not only a person who has attained a high level of internal self-discovery and purity, but also a person who is well versed in the scriptural writings and has knowledge of parables and myths along with their mystical implications. He or she also knows the practices which lead a person to spiritual evolution (Yoga disciplines).

If the teaching is given directly it may be misunderstood or even repudiated altogether due to the state of mind of the individual. Hence, the student must be properly initiated into the teaching and the proper relationship must be established between teacher and student.

The teacher offers humility and honesty with a beguiling wit, cheerfulness and an uplifting outlook. This is symbolized by the divine food Djehuti offered Hetheru. The teacher brings divine food in the form of wisdom teachings which uplift the mind by relieving the burden of pain and sorrow which weighs down the soul of a human being due to ignorance and negativity. The divine food is the taste of divine glory. It is a glimpse of the goal which a disciple must aspire to experience in its fullness. However, this fullness is experienced in degrees as the teacher gives the spiritual teaching and as it is assimilated by the student.

The student must learn to respect and trust the teacher. Also, the student must allow the teaching to penetrate deeply within the heart. It is only then that the teaching will have a transformative effect. Hetheru allowed Djehuti's words to penetrate her cold, anguished heart. Then she began to remember her past glory. This is the process of divine memory wherein she began to regain the remembrance of her true identity. The pain of seeing her current level of existence in comparison with her past glory brought her to tears. Also, she felt the pain of realizing that she was missing out on the boundless divine love of her father. This is the common emotional experience of a spiritual aspirant when understanding as to their true predicament begins to dawn. "What have I done to come down from the heights of divinity to the limited state of human life and mortal existence? How wretched am I? How degraded am I?" These are the kinds of questions asked by a spiritual aspirant before he / she begins to understand the meaning of the spiritual teachings. This form of thinking leads to a resolution to regain one's true glory and to rise up from the degradation of ignorance, "May I find a teacher who can guide me on the path to self-discovery and enlightenment at once!" Thus, Hetheru, came to respect Djehuti. She accepted his offering, listened to his teaching and later trusted him with her life. As one begins to reflect on the teaching, intuitional understanding opens up the opportunity to view the beauty and experience the infinite compassion of the Self. Then there are no more questions, only a keen desire to experience this elevated state more and more. An aspirant might say at this point, "I have glimpsed a wondrous bliss within. Let me fully discover it and abide in it."

The first parable imparted the understanding of *Maat* or righteous action and the glory of the Divine. Maat is the order, justice and righteousness of the universe. It is the law of cause and effect set up by the Divine to maintain harmony in the universe. Any action performed will bring a reaction to the person performing the action. Thus, positive actions set up a positive karmic basis for positive occurences in a person's life. Negative actions set up a negative karmic basis for negative occurences to happen in a person's life. It may not be right away but it will occur at some point in time. Therefore, it is important to hold pure thoughts and perform good deeds in order to promote goodness, peace and harmony in your life. What you do comes back to you! This is the Ancient Egyptian ***Principle of Meskhenet*** (popularly known as The Law of Karma in modern culture).

The goddesses *Shai* (fate or destiny), *Rennenet* (fortune) and *Meskhenet* together form the principle of cause and effect which determines a person's future in accordance with their actions, beliefs, feelings and desires, their karmic basis. Therefore, these deities (cosmic forces set up by the Divine) decree whether or not a person will move forward and attain oneness with the Divine or if the person will move backwards and experience degraded states of mind. They determine the next birth (family, country, circumstance, etc.) of an individual. The important thing to understand is that they do not determine a person's fate or destiny. They only carry out the sum total of a person's karmic will.

A person's karmic will is their unconscious resolve based on their accumulated desires, beliefs and feelings by which a person has lived, the karmic basis. So if a person desires wealth and carries out various actions in an attempt to gain wealth they set up a basis for seeking wealth. These actions become stored in the unconscious mind as impressions and at the time of death they impel a person to continue searching for wealth in an unconscious way. If a person was evil in life their own karmic basis will send them to a plane of consciousness where they will experience evil. This is known as Hell. If a person was a performer of good deeds in life their own karmic basis will send them to a plane of consciousness where they will experience heavenly conditions. This is known as Heaven.

If the person could not attain some desire in the present lifetime, Meskhenet will cause that person to be reborn in a country, family and circumstance where they will be able to continue pursuing that desire (karmic will). This form of desiring things which are ultimately perishable becomes the basis for reincarnation. Heaven and hell are not permanent states of being for the soul. Like the physical world and human life, heaven and hell are relative states. All relative states of experience are transitory. They all come to an end. The only state of being that is permanent and, imperishable is when the mind is enlightened and the eternal Divine Self is discovered. This is because all desires and the entire karmic basis dissolves. Enlightenment dissolves the karmic basis because it is made up of illusions, desires, passions and ignorance. Since spiritual practice and enlightenment eradicates ignorance and illusions, there are no desires left for that which is negative or for the ephemeral pleasures and attainments of mortal existence. If a person was a practitioner of Yoga in life, their own purified karmic basis will send them to expand beyond desires and to discover the Divine Self. This is known as spiritual enlightenment, liberation, eternal freedom, immortality, etc. Only this attainment ends the cycle of birth and death (reincarnation, going back into a body in order to experience physical human existence once again).

Therefore, spiritual philosophy directs a spiritual aspirant to desire after that which is not perishable and fleeting, the Divine Self. So it is important to understand that a person can control his or her own fate by controlling their desires, thoughts and feelings. These put together comprise what is referred to as "mind" in mystical philosophy. Therefore, control of the mind is the most important aspect of spiritual practice because the mind determines everything that happens in life, whether it be positive or negative. Mind is the cause of experiences of hell or heaven, happiness or sorrow, enlightenment or degradation, etc.

Even the most infinitesimal forms of life in the universe cannot escape this karmic law. Therefore, a spiritual aspirant must learn to desire what is true and to act according to what is good and righteous. The karmic law is an example of the power and glory of the Divine Self (Ra). Even more wonderful is the realization that every living being is a part of the intricate fabric of life and that all are looked after by the Supreme Being, no matter how insignificant they may seem to be. Another important teaching here is that no one can do an unrighteous act and get away with it. At some point (in the present life or in a future life) they will reap the effects of their unrighteous action of the past in the form of misfortune, adversity, disappointment and frustrations. Punishment is meted for all those who transgress the universal laws of life which include compassion, honesty, justice, righteousness, peace and universal love.

So the law of karma says that for every cause there will be an effect. In addition, the cause and the effect will be of equal intensity. Also, the effect will be the cause transformed. The problem arises because the majority of people do not have proper insight into this law. Most people do not even believe that they are the only person responsible for the situations that befall them in life, good or bad. However, they are usually more willing to take credit for the good things that happen to them than the bad things. This problem is compounded because often the cause and the effect do not look identical, and do not occur one right after the other. For example, if you plant a seed of a sweet fruit (i.e. date), you will reap sweet fruits. However, if you planted the seed of a sour fruit (i.e. lime), you will reap only sour fruits. So, you will reap the results of whatever thoughts and actions you put out into the world. This reaping is carried over into future lifetimes. However, neither the seed of the date or lime look like the actual fruit it brought forth. If you were only to see the fruit (effect), you may not be able to describe the exact way the seed which was planted (cause) looked. Likewise, most people have no insight into the cause of the negative effect they are currently experiencing in their lives. Therefore, the tendency in modern society is to blame someone or something outside of oneself for any adversity which befalls one. The purpose of having insight into this law is not to blame yourself for your current adverse situations and wallow in self-pity, but to realize that as you created the situation due to ignorant (egoistic) behavior in the past, you can un-create it through righteous thoughts and actions in the present. You are not stuck in your situation indefinitely. Through your righteous self-effort you have every possibility of working to make your situation better. Therefore the purpose of thoroughly understanding the law of cause and effect (Maat philosophy) is to become self-empowered, and not to feel that you are a poor victim of life's cruel whims who has no control over their destiny.

Following the first parable, Djehuti introduces the teachings related to the Creation of the universe. He explains to Hetheru that the land of Egypt was created by her father (Ra) from a Primeval Ocean which was formless in the beginning, and that it is a land of many wonders and incomparable beauty. This description is a mystical way of relating the nature of Creation and the glory of the entity who created it. Then Djehuti begins to show her that the splendor of the Supreme Being is also her own splendor and glory. He begins to relate her to the divine glory that is latent within herself and to bolster her pride in her own heritage. He imparts to her the feeling of goodness that is the Divine. He relates how her absence left a great void in Creation, causing pain and sorrow to all people. Every life form has a place in Creation.

Also, every life form is loved by God, who manifests his love in the form of relatives, acquaintances and nature itself. So all people have a purpose in life and their existence is meaningful. Also, they are cared for by the Divine Self in various forms. The highest purpose is to discover your true identity and find your own place which has been degreed for you by the Supreme Divinity.

THE CREATION

The process of Creation is explained in the form of a cosmological system for better understanding. Cosmology is a branch of philosophy dealing with the origin, processes and structure of the universe. Cosmogony is the astrophysical study of the Creation and evolution of the universe. Both of these disciplines are inherent facets of Egyptian philosophy through the main religious systems or Companies of the gods and goddesses. A company of gods and goddesses is a group of deities which symbolize a particular cosmic force or principle which emanates from the all-encompassing Supreme Being, from which they have emerged. The Self or Supreme Being manifests Creation through the properties and principles represented by the *Pautti* (Company of gods and goddesses-cosmic laws of nature). The system or company of gods and goddesses of Anu is regarded as the oldest, and forms the basis of the Osirian Trinity. It is expressed in the diagram below.

Ra-Tem
⇩
Hetheru
Tehuti
Maat
⇩
Shu ⇔ Tefnut
⇩
Geb ⇔ Nut

Set — Nebthet   ↖   Asar ⇔ Aset   ↘   Asar ⇔ Nebthet
⇩   ⇩
Heru   Apuat

The diagram above shows that *Pautti*, the creative principles which are embodied in the primordial gods and goddesses of Creation, emanated from the Supreme Being. Ra or Ra-Tem arose out of the "Nu," the Primeval waters, the hidden essence, and began sailing the *"Boat of Millions of Years"* which included the company of gods and goddesses. On his boat emerged the "Neteru" or cosmic principles of Creation. The neters of the Pautti are Ra-Atum, Shu, Tefnut, Geb, Nut, Asar, Aset, Set, and Nebthet. Hetheru, Djehuti and Maat represent attributes of the Supreme Being as the very *stuff* or *substratum* which makes up Creation. Shu, Tefnut, Geb, Nut, Asar (Osiris), Aset (Isis), Set, and Nebthet (Nephthys) represent the principles upon which Creation manifests. Apuat or Anpu is not part of the Ennead. He represents the feature of intellectual discrimination in the Osirian myth. "Sailing" signifies the beginning of motion in Creation. Motion implies that events occur in the realm of time and space, thus, the phenomenal universe comes into existence as a mass of moving essence we call the elements. Prior to this motion, there was the primeval state of being without any form and without existence in time or space.

Hetheru began to cry upon realizing what she seemed to have lost and forgotten. Then a strange thing happened. Djehuti tried to get her to return to Egypt and all of a sudden she realized what he was doing and she fell back into the pit of negativity. This is not an uncommon occurrence in spiritual life or in ordinary life. Sometimes a person may experience joy, and then seemingly for no reason they may fall into the pits of depression. Sometimes the mental delusion and the erupting emotions cause a person to strike out with anger in an uncontrolled manner, even towards those who offer them kindness or the truth. This is a factor caused by negative impressions in the karmic basis from the past. Anger, hatred and rage are forms of mental illness and their intensity most times incapacitates a person's faculties of reasoning self-control. At this time, understanding, gentleness, forgiveness and humility, but most of all patience are needed in order to deal with people who are in this degraded, dull state of mind.

Djehuti is the embodiment of patience and the wellspring of parables (mystical wisdom teachings). So he wisely humbles himself and begs for mercy. He seemingly submits to her power and does not attempt to confront it since he is no match for her might. At the same time he cleverly captivates her attention away from anger and violence and channels her feelings towards interest in another mystical parable. An important point in dealing with the dull mind is how the negative thoughts and feelings are handled. It is important to view the negative thoughts and feelings as well as the adverse conditions of life as challenges to be overcome instead of as feeling that one is a victim of negativity from others or from one's own mistakes. The former idea is empowering because a person who practices it will not allow the negativity to make them upset. When the mind is not upset it can it can endure the negativity, understanding that it will not last forever, while at the same time think clearly and resolve the problems. Also, it is very important when in dull state of mind that one does not simply say, "I will wait until the negativity passes over before I do any work" or try to figure out where the negativity came from, because these tactics will only serve to increase the negativity. Suppose you have a hole in the ground you want to go away. If keep digging the hole, believing that it will either go away or you will be able to find out where it comes from, you will only make the hole bigger. A mind, clouded by agitation and distress, will lead itself into deeper and deeper pits of despair, anguish and sorrow with no resolution in view. The only way to fix the hole is by bringing fresh dirt and filling it. Likewise, when you have the hole of negativity in your consciousness, you must fill it with something opposite to effect a change. So the scriptures recommend the disciplines of prayer, selfless service, repetition of the Divine Name, reflection on scriptural teachings to channel the negative emotions in a positive direction, as exemplified by this story.

Goddess Worship and Rituals of Enlightenment

In addition, the teaching itself must be presented in a manner to which the aspirant can relate. This objective is accomplished through the use of myths, parables, stories, similes and metaphors which are directly relevant to an individual's cultural experience and their human experience. *Listening to the teachings* is the first and most important step in imparting the spiritual teachings. Therefore, many intriguing, fascinating and beguiling ways have been devised by the Sages to transmit the teachings that captivate the attention of the listener. Myths and parables have very important features. They are easier to recall, and have a more direct impact on the untrained mind than direct mystical philosophy because they are easy to identify with, as opposed to proverbs or aphorisms which contain raw spiritual truths that require a well trained mind in order to be grasped and appreciated. The next step in the process of learning the teachings it *reflecting* upon them. This implies the continuous study and practice of the teachings. As you read over a spiritual text and practice its wisdom in your life, deeper and deeper aspects of the teaching will reveal itself to you, purifying your heart in greater and greater degrees. The next step in learning the teachings is *meditating* upon them. Meditation implies going deep within your mind to a level which is beyond thoughts. It is discovering the *intuitional* level of mind. The correct understanding of the teachings and their continuous practice in day to day life will automatically lead a person to the meditative state in the course of time. This level of mind is also known in Ancient Egyptian terminology as *Nrutef,* the place where there are no thoughts or vibrations. This practice means communing with the absolute Self within you which is beyond your thoughts, desires and sentimental feelings.

The second parable reinforces the teaching of Ra's omniscience. Hetheru was able to develop *devotion towards the Divine.* Devotion towards the Divine is an important development in spiritual life. It means channeling one's emotions towards what is true, beautiful and good and turning away from that which is erroneous, illusory and the source of pain and sorrow in life. So devotion to God means turning away from the sentimental desires of the ego and turning the feelings toward the Divine. Devotion and wisdom are closely related. Each fulfills the other and together they lead a spiritual aspirant to discover the Higher Self. In order to love something, you must learn about it. The Divine Self is no exception. The blossoming devotion in Hetheru's heart (love for God) and the teaching of Djehuti about the wisdom of the Self allowed Hetheru to calm down and to see the infinite glory of the Divine Self. His teachings revealed the hierarchical order of living beings in Creation, and also the idea that even the most powerful living beings are all under the control of and ultimately answer to the Supreme Self.

Djehuti presents the character of the Sefer (griffin) in the role of divine avenger or the divinity who enforces the divine law. The griffin is a mythological animal encompassing the body of a lion, the head and wings of a hawk, and the tail of a lion or a serpent. In legends from India, the Far East and ancient Scythia, griffins were known as the guardians of treasures and mines. In Greek mythology they drew the carriage or chariot of the sun and were the guardians of gold treasures. In this parable the Sefer (griffin) represents the supreme instrument or power of the Divine. In reality, this is Hetheru's true identity as the Eye of Ra. This is why Djehuti created an elaborate story detailing the hierarchy of creatures and showing how none can escape from the power of the Sefer. So in a subtle and indirect way he is teaching her about herself throughout the story. At the end of the parable he reveals to her that she has this same power and that she herself is the Eye of Ra which has power over all creatures. Thus, he introduces her to her own higher nature in a clever and artistic manner.

Another important teaching presented to Hetheru in the first two parables was that of *faith.* The teaching showed her how God exists in the very fabric of Creation. In fact all Creation has proceeded from God and every part of Creation is permeated by God's presence. His fairness and compassion is evident in the principles of righteousness, fortune, destiny and cause and effect (Maat, Rennenet, Shai and Meskhenet) which sustain Creation. In order to receive this teaching, she needed to develop faith in her teacher. This enabled her to listen and reflect upon the teaching instead of rejecting the teachings and killing the teacher.

The third parable has important implications for spiritual life. Hetheru has now turned away from the pit of negativity, the dull state of mind, but she is not free from the delusion of ignorance which is rooted deep within her heart. She still remains in the form of a wildcat and even though she has had certain glimpses of the divine glory of her Higher Self, she is still partially entangled in the lower self as well. This is the predicament of many people. They have some inkling of their higher spiritual essence but they are caught up in the egoism which still remains in the form of ignorance, lower desires and wrong thinking. It must be cleansed from their minds. This state is known as *agitation of mind.* It is characterized by impure thoughts and feelings based on ignorance of the higher spiritual reality, and on indulgence in egoistic feelings, selfishness and individuality. When the mind is agitated it cannot understand or feel clearly. The thoughts and feelings are tainted with illusion and desire. This is why, when strong emotions and feelings take control of the mind, the mind cannot reason objectively. Likewise, when people are deeply involved in worldly activities with an egoistic intent, they are actually moving away from self-discovery and intensifying the illusions, distractions, and worldly desires in their minds. It is like going to the beach and staying at the surface, being aware only of the waves, and never going down below the surface to experience the peace and calm below. Conversely, when a person lives in accordance with the teaching and affirms the spiritual reality in all areas of life, working to promote harmony, peace and truth in their life, they are moving closer to self-discovery. They may have an active life and still experience inner peace and the divine presence. This is the ideal.

When the mind is calm it can see the truth clearly and one's ideas about oneself also become clear as well. A person may feel great in the morning, full of anticipation and cheerfulness because they believe they will make money that day. So the mind is agitated with the expectation of making money and the myriad of things they will do with it. They are not thinking about the possibility of not getting what they want. This person has deluded himself or herself into expecting a desire to be fulfilled. In the afternoon the expectation is not met so the frustration sets in and depression ensues. They become angry and belligerent because they have attached themselves to the roller coaster of emotions and egoistic expectation based on the activities they perform in the world of human experience. They are detached from the world of the spirit, so they have no awareness of the higher reality. They are like a boat caught up in a storm, going up with elation and down with depression, with no end in sight. They miss out on the more profound positive feeling which lies below the waves of elation and depression. When one steadies the mind, not allowing it to become dejected (to the capacity that one can do so) or elated (again to one;s capacity), one experiences the depths of their true being. This is the practice of keeping the scales of Maat balanced. In this steadiness of mind they will experience an expansion in consciousness and enjoy a more profound experience of happiness, called bliss, and peace, called hetep. This the bliss and peace of this expansion in consciousness is experienced in greater and greater degrees by an initiate or aspirant who practices keeping the mind calm at all times. It is really what people are trying acquire by continuously trying to arrange situations which will make they feel good (elated) and escape from situations which make them feel bad (dejection, depression). However, because they settle for either for elation if they can arrange the situation or dejection if they cannot (both of which cause mental agitation), they never get to experience that which they are really seeking, true happiness (bliss) and peace of mind (hetep). The experience of the happiness which is termed elation is like one drop of water in the ocean as compared to the whole ocean which is experienced when the mind attains the state of perfect serenity and enlightenment dawns on that individual. So the masses of people, feeling that by pursuing the sensual pleasures of life they are being good to themselves, are in reality short changing themselves. They are being miserly with themselves, settling for so little, when in fact with a little discipline and self-effort they can have so much. Agitation arises from desires. Desires exist in the mind because it is searching to fulfil a deep longing for wholeness. The mind is erroneously operating based on the concept that acquiring something, entering into a relationship with someone or experiencing some kind of pleasure will fulfill the need, but all activities in the relative world cannot satisfy the need because all activities there are transitory and the mind itself is transitory. It is not possible to experience abiding peace, happiness and joy with something that is transitory, unpredictable and impermanent (ever-changing).

A spiritual aspirant learns to understand the hollowness* of emotions and the futility of worry, pleasure-seeking, wealth, fame and sentimental egoistic values of society and popular culture. A spiritual aspirant is not caught up in them nor does an aspirant indulge in expectations and desires based on illusion. Instead an aspirant pursues reason and truth. Impure thoughts may not necessarily be evil thoughts. They can be based on ignorance alone even if their outcome appears to be evil. The root cause of impurity in the mind is ignorance of the Higher Self. Examples of impure thoughts may be, "I am alone in this world and nobody cares for me," or "I am a miserable human being and there may be a God but he does not care for me," or "life is for pleasure and I will get mine any way I can and I don't care about anyone else," or "life has no purpose so I don't care whether I live or die." *(void, desolation, emptiness.)

A spiritual aspirant must learn to think positively, keep the mind steady in pleasure and pain by surrendering when one's expectations are not met and have positive expectations and desires. These will lead to freedom from negativity and ultimately to the experience of enlightenment. A positive desire is to desire to become pure of heart and a positive expectation is to look forward to the experience of discovering God. These are in accord with the teachings and serve to fulfill the purpose (goal) of human life. Other examples of positive desires are desires to help humanity and nature, visit spiritual centers or read spiritual texts.

The spiritual teaching shows the fallacy of ignorant and egoistic thinking and the manner in which it degrades the mind to the extent of causing people to act callously and selfishly. When a person acts in negative ways he or she is in reality going against the inner nature, the higher truth deep down. This acts as a poison in one's mind and body which manifests as physical or mental diseases such as agitation, restlessness, arguing nature, selfishness, etc. When the problem becomes acute, advanced mental and physical diseases arise such as schizophrenia, dementia, delusions, hallucinations, ulcers, cancers, etc. Ultimately, the affliction of negativity in the mind leads to the disease of negative karma, hellish conditions and reincarnation.

So Djehuti tells Hetheru the parable of the two jackals who were spared by the lion because of their *calmness and truthfulness*. As previously discussed, calmness is an important quality for a spiritual aspirant. It implies remaining balanced in the time when there is temptation or when there is disturbance in the environment. It means maintaining an equal vision towards all things and not letting one's emotions hold sway when a decision needs to be made. It means controlling the emotions and desires and not allowing them to control one's life. It means living in accordance with truth and reason and holding fast to correct action even when the mind and body desires something else. In Ancient Egyptian Maat Philosophy,* this practice is referred to as "keeping the balance." Calmness of mind implies developing equal vision or impartiality. This means not being affected by the ever-changing situations and circumstances of life, be they positive or negative. It means cultivating positive desires and then remaining centered in one's own self, neither expecting fulfillment of desires nor expecting that they will not be fulfilled, but surrendering to the divine will who knows what is best. It is the art of remaining neutral in all conditions and knowing that the Divine will provide the appropriate result for all actions performed. This discipline also involves drawing inner satisfaction from a job well done and allowing the Divine to flow through you for the betterment of all humanity instead of looking to fulfil a personal desire or receive a fruit or reward for what you have done. The discipline of calmness means remaining balanced when things are going well, and also when they do not seem to be going well, knowing that God has everything well in hand and that whatever the outcome may be, you will never lose God, eternity and immortality. It is understanding that even if the Divine Self brings you some situation that appears to be negative, that it is ultimately for your greater benefit and spiritual enlightenment. A person who has advanced in calming the mind can experience oneness with God, the source of peace and bliss, at any time and in any place. *See the book *The Wisdom of Maati* by Dr. Muata Ashby.

Truthfulness is important because life is meaningless without it. Without truth, nothing real can be known. If a person lives their life in accordance with ignorance and egoism, everything they experience will be an illusion. Consequently they will never be able to discover true happiness and inner peace. For example, most people believe that if they win a lottery they will be happy. This is an ignorant understanding. Their wealth gained from the lottery will only lead to more mental agitation (elation, greed) and frustrations later on. They will only be happy for a short period of time, because even one lifetime is short as compared to eternity. In addition, they are creating false impressions in their unconscious as to the source of true happiness. Consequently, in their future lifetimes, they will be very unhappy whenever they find themselves without lots of money. It is so important that an aspirant make every effort to understand that the only source of happiness is the Self. And even when your spiritual aspiration is not strong enough to prevent you from deluding yourself and you find yourself elated as a result of having acquired some object or situation in the world of time and space, remind yourself that the source of that happiness you are experiencing is due to the Self, and not the object. Also reflect on the spiritual teachings which tells you that the happiness which you experience as a result of some happening in the world is like one drop as compared to the ocean of happiness that awaits you when you attain Enlightenment. Then and only then will you discover true happiness and true wealth. The happiness that objects and situations offer is like a mirage. No sooner do you attain it and experience it for a short time than it just vanishes into thin air, leaving you feeling insecure and miserable. You must continuously reflect that true happiness comes from discovering the Higher Self who is infinite peace, immortal, eternal and has the power to overcome all obstacles.

The fourth parable relates to *humility*. Humility is a quality that should not be confused with humiliation. It is an advanced quality which allows a person to rise above the lower self by sublimating the negative aspects of the ego. Think about it. You may know people or may even recognize yourself acting in egoistic ways based on pride in your own physical prowess, strength, beauty, possessions, fame, etc. These egoistic patterns have been developed as you grew up in society and accepted its values which emphasize physical beauty, sexuality, fame, wealth and so on. But if these values are correct, why is it that the people who have the most money, fame, opportunity for sex relations, plastic surgery and notoriety in the world are not the happiest people in the world? Why is it that they are susceptible to the same failings, misfortunes and calamities as all other people? There is a great illusion in popular society that most people follow without examining closely, that there is some situation, possession or person in the world that can bring them happiness. People have been searching for such an object since the beginning of time, without any success. Hetheru had searched for it in vain. Now she realized that what she was searching for was something she already had within herself. No person or living creature can escape Meskhenet or the jaws of death. This must be clearly understood.

Your ego is not a real part of your personality. It is an illusion which you are sustaining due to an error in understanding your true Higher Self. Your ego, meaning your personality, sense organs, physical body and thoughts are in reality transient aspects of yourself. They are instruments that the soul uses in order to have experiences in the world of time and space. They are not absolute realities. This is why at the time of death, the unenlightened soul sheds the personality and ego and moves on to other experiences. It will reincarnate at some point in the future and use a new ego personality, just as a person may change clothing. When you act in accordance with righteousness you are also putting down the ego. When the ego is not given prominence in the personality it becomes an instrument instead of an obstruction. It becomes a servant instead of a slave master who forces a person to enter into situations and entanglements which at the beginning seem to promise happiness, but which later will lead to great pain and sorrow.

When a person overlooks performing correct action in favor of indulging in the personal desires, their actions will be based on egoism. All actions tainted with egoism will inevitably lead to disappointment and frustration at some point in the future. Therefore, the inability to act in accordance with truth must be understood as a defect in the personality, a mental illness. It is the illness of **delusion**. Delusion is intensified by activities which bolster the ego, spiritual ignorance and the egoistic desires. So the pleasure-seeking mentality, the pursuit of sensual pleasures, the desire to possess objects, wealth, fame and power for personal aggrandizement are all examples of egoistic desires which lead to delusion and mental agitation.

The spiritual teaching allows a person to discover a higher form of fulfillment. It allows a person to understand the underlying basis of Creation, and the illusoriness of desiring fleeting egoistic pursuits and perishable objects. You need to have some relationships and possessions in the course of a normal life. However, you should never hold onto anything in the world even as you are experiencing it and possessing it. Your possessions and relationships should be based on righteousness and truth, and never on ostentatiousness, greed and lust.

The spiritual lifestyle allows a spiritual aspirant to go beyond the erroneous desires, thoughts and feelings that cause agitation of the mind. It shows a person how to calm the mind. When the mind is calmed it becomes clear just as a lake becomes clear when the waves subside. This calmness or serenity of mind allows the real essence of a person to become visible and the ego becomes transparent. When the mind is cleansed, the Divine Self comes into clear view as the reality sustaining the ego. When the mind is purified, devoid of the pressure of desires and illusions, one reaches a state of harmony with the universe. This state of consciousness which a person experiences when the mind is serene is referred to as **lucidity of mind.** Lucidity is the quality which is characterized by detachment from the ego and identification with the Higher Self, God. Therefore, lucidity of mind is the objective of all spiritual disciplines because it leads to spiritual enlightenment (self-knowledge) and freedom from ignorance, egoism and negative karma. A person who is lucid is free from attachments and internally fulfilled. He or she expresses goodwill towards all and displays a **gentle nature**. This was Hetheru's condition when she entered the city of Waset.

It is notable that Hetheru was a vicious beast when she was in the states of dullness and agitation, but then she reverted back to her true form when she became gentle, kind and calm. This points to the fact that the source of ugliness and negativity within the human personality lies in the state of mind which a person adopts. The mindset which a person adopts is in accordance with their level of spiritual evolution.

Therefore, ignorance and delusion lead to ugliness and negativity in the form of anger, hatred, greed, selfishness, jealousy, conflict, frustration and violence. On the other hand, serenity and lucidity of mind lead to the expression of peace, gentleness, compassion, love and other virtuous qualities in one's personality.

Detachment from the ego should not be a hard concept to understand. Most people's concept of self is based on their identification with the ego. This is because the ego and its desires, longings and beliefs are all that the person understands. However, spiritual practice allows a person to discover the underlying essence of the mind. This occurs to every person in the world every single day of their lives, albeit indirectly. When you go to sleep you experience dreams but at other times there are no dreams and no awareness of the world. What happened to your ego? It dissolved into your consciousness just as a wave subsides into the ocean from which it arises. When you wake up you feel refreshed. You experience a transcendental feeling, but do not specifically remember what happened. What would happen if you were to cause the waves of thoughts and egoistic desires to subside while you were in the state of wakefulness? You would discover, in a conscious way, the same truth that you experience in deep dreamless sleep. You would discover that there is a deeper part of yourself which sustains your personality and day to day realities. It is this deeper essence of who you are that manifests as the three states of consciousness (dullness, agitation and lucidity) and the seven manifestations of psycho-spiritual consciousness (energy centers). This is your Higher Self, that part of you which is not dependent on the world and the desires of the ego. When you discover and abide in this state of consciousness you are freed from the lower states. You become an enlightened Sage, a knower of the true meaning of the teachings and the monarch or ruler over every aspect of your personality. You become supremely peaceful, *hetep,* and you rise above all temptations and all illusions. The Higher Self is to be discovered by the following plan as presented in the story of Hetheru and Djehuti. They have been discussed at length throughout this gloss and are presented summarily below. Even though the principles from *The Story of Hetheru and Djehuti* have been presented below as a succession in a hierarchical order, all of these disciplines are best practiced in an integral fashion. This means that you do not wait to perfect Maat before starting to practice detachment. You should practice all of these as life presents you with opportunities to test your spiritual strength or Hetheru faculty.

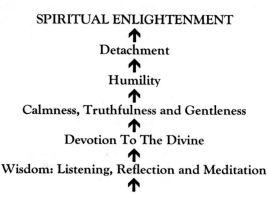

SPIRITUAL ENLIGHTENMENT

⬆

Detachment

⬆

Humility

⬆

Calmness, Truthfulness and Gentleness

⬆

Devotion To The Divine

⬆

Wisdom: Listening, Reflection and Meditation

⬆

Mysticism of the Ancient Egyptian Goddess

Reference and respect for the Spiritual Teacher

↑

Preceptorship - Association with an authentic Spiritual Teacher

↑

Practice Maat and live in accordance with the Principle of Meskhenet

↑

Spiritual Ignorance: Dullness and Agitation

An ordinary person needs to enjoy the company of another person or experience some situation in time and space to feel joy and happiness. This is the difference between an un-enlightened person and a person who is advancing spiritually. A person who has experienced the absolute state of consciousness can remember the experience and feel unobstructed bliss and joy. This act of recalling the experience of the Divine is known as remembrance of God. When the feeling of oneness with the Divine becomes a perpetual experience, that state is referred to as spiritual enlightenment or achieving oneness with the Divine. Ordinary people experience tiny and transient glimpses of this bliss and joy in daily life as happiness and elation. However, they ascribe it to some object they acquired, some person in their life or some situation they saw as beneficial. Others experience joy spontaneously for no apparent reason, but it fades away as mysteriously as it came. A Sage (practitioner of Yoga) learns to discover the source of bliss and unobstructed joy and to abide there continuously by not allowing egoistic desires, expectations, sentimentality, anger, hatred, greed, etc. to cloud their experience. The unobstructed experience of joy and peace is what all living things are striving for in various ways, even if they do not realize it. Therefore, it is said that an enlightened Sage has accomplished the most important task in life, achieving which, nothing is left to be achieve. Therefore, they direct their energy to the spiritual upliftment of humanity.

The character of Djehuti and his relationship to Hetheru implies another important teaching in relation to the teacher-student relationship. An advanced spiritual teacher does not see him or herself as the originator of the teaching. It is God who is working through them to bring the teaching forth for the benefit of all humanity. People often ask where God is when bad things are happening and why there is no one to help in time of need. People need to understand that God is everywhere, especially in the heart of authentic spiritual preceptors and in the good intentions of others. However, people need to purify their hearts, because an impure heart that is constantly producing negative thoughts and feelings will not be able to recognize an authentic spiritual preceptor or the good intentions of others. Such a mind will become like poison, killing the vision of goodness in life. Consequently, such dull personalities will constantly lead themselves into negative situations and relationships. Thus, their negative mind set and actions will lead them to experiences which seemingly reinforce their own erroneous beliefs. They would not benefit from the teachings of even the greatest spiritual teachers such as Djehuti, Aset, Jesus, Buddha, etc. Such personalities will have to go through many incarnations where they will eventually learn to follow the precepts of Maat. Therefore, the compassion of the Goddess is so great that she has come to the world in the form of the scriptural

46

writings, compassion and the spirit of service in the human heart, Sages, Saints and the high mystical philosophy and religious iconography.

There is also a mystical significance to the rejoicing in the cities when Hetheru returned to her rightful place. The cities mentioned, Anu, Het-ku-Ptah and Waset, relate to cities of the gods of the great Ancient Egyptian Trinity of *Amun-Ra-Ptah*. The Ancient Egyptian Hymns of Amun contain the key to understanding the mystical meaning of the teaching. The Ancient Egyptian teaching "Neberdjer-Amun-Ra-Ptah" is explained as follows. Neberdjer means the "Supreme Being." Amun-Ra-Ptah represent the triune manner in which the Supreme Being manifests Creation. Amun represents witnessing consciousness or self-awareness. Ra represents the cosmic mind which sustains all mental activity and is the means for consciousness to interact with Creation, the light or power of consciousness. Ptah represents the physical universe with which the witnessing consciousness interacts. This triad is also related to human life. All human beings have three bodies, the physical, astral and causal. The soul in every human being is like a spark of the Self, Neberdjer, who uses these bodies in order to have experiences in the varied forms of life in Creation.

The Trinity also relates to the human mind. The mind of a human being experiences three states of awareness, waking, dream and dreamless sleep, as well as three modes of manifestation, "dullness, agitation and lucidity." Thus, the return of Hetheru signifies the rejoicing in all aspects of a person's personality, the emotions, intellect, will and physical nature. This is, of course, a description of a human being who has attained spiritual perfection.

The seven day festivity relates to the seven centers of psycho-spiritual consciousness. Hetheru is the goddess of the seven aspects of consciousness in her form as the seven divine Hetheru cows. The one Supreme Being in the form of a bull (Asar-Osiris), expresses in seven modes of consciousness (the seven cows). This expression of the spirit is symbolized by Hetheru in her seven aspects. Hetheru represents divine consciousness emanating from the Divine Self (Eye of Ra emanating from the Sun). She (divine consciousness) expresses herself (itself) as the essence which sustains the mind of every human being as well. Every human being has seven psycho-spiritual consciousness centers in their astral body. These act as transducers of psychic energy from the soul level of consciousness. They sustain the physical body. Each center relates to an aspect of human personality. As a person develops, the *Arat* or the Serpent Power energy (Inner Life Force known as Kundalini in India or Chi in China) of the goddess, these energy centers are cleansed and their power is allowed to unfold. Thus, a human being evolves spiritually through the power of the goddess. The Serpent Power automatically awakens when a person studies and practices the teachings. However, the process of raising one's spiritual power may be aided by specific exercises such as concentration, proper breathing, righteous action, devotion to the Divine, meditation on the meanings of the spiritual symbols and surrendering to the will of the Higher Self (God). These techniques allow a person to transform their waking personality so that they may discover their innermost Self: God. For more on the Serpent Power and the techniques for cultivating it see the book "The Serpent Power" by Dr. Muata Ashby.

A GLOSS ON THE MYTH OF RA AND ASET

In the Ausarian Resurrection story, Asar and his reincarnation in the form of Heru is a symbol for the resurrection which must occur in the life of every human being. In this manner, the story of the Ausarian Trinity of Asar, Aset and Heru and the Egyptian Psedjet holds hidden teachings, which when understood and properly practiced, will lead to spiritual enlightenment.

So Aset is the true heroine of the entire myth relating to Asar. It was because of Aset's love, devotion and knowledge of how to call on the Divine (Ra) that Heru, the redeemer of righteousness upon earth, was resurrected.

So what was this special nature of this goddess which allowed her to resurrect Asar and Heru, and what is the significance of this resurrection? What relation does it have to people in modern times?

The story of Ra and Aset, though short, imparts important mystical teachings of monumental proportions. First we are introduced to the Supreme Being in the form of Ra. Ra is the essence of all Creation, the mover in motion, the wetness of water, the heat in the sun's rays, the sustaining force in the air that allows living beings to live by breath. Ra is the very root from which all emanates and is sustained. Ra sits on his barque which emerged from the Primeval Ocean. Waves form as a result of the movement of his barque. These waves are vibrations which cause all of the differentiation of matter in the world. All matter, the world itself, is essentially the Primeval Ocean, after its constituent elements have taken forms due to the vibrations produced from the motion of the barque of Ra. If Ra ceases to move in his barque the matter of the universe will be devoid of vibration and will return to an undifferentiated form.

Aset is the female manifestation of Ra. She is his daughter. Aset lived as a woman, but she evolved by learning the knowledge of the world. This knowledge is sometimes referred to as the lower mysteries. It relates to information about the physical world, human interaction and human life. Sciences such as engineering, medicine, anthropology, history, social interactions, politics, economics, etc., are related to human beings and to the relative world. They are changeable and subject to error. The use of the word "relative" here implies the understanding that all worldly knowledge has a practical value as long as the world exists, and as long as there is human life. However, what sciences were there before the world and human beings came into existence and which sciences will be there after the world and human beings cease to exist? The answer is none. Further, what use is science to someone who is asleep or dead? The answer is none. Therefore, worldly knowledge which is related to events in time and space are only useful in a particular reality, a particular realm of existence, and not in all places and at all times. Therefore it is referred to as relative, and as practical knowledge.

Goddess Worship and Rituals of Enlightenment

Aset developed an interest in discovering the higher truths and realities. This quality is termed *spiritual aspiration*. She wanted to discover the truth which is not conditional or relative, but that which is absolute and eternal. Absolute truth is real truth because it is not affected by time or circumstance. She knew that Ra was the higher truth because he was the Creator of the relative universe. So she began to meditate on the idea of discovering the name of her father since this was the highest truth of all.

The "mystical name" is an Ancient Egyptian philosophy which relates to understanding the essence of a thing. Everything that comes into existence receives a name, and then this thing is "known." However, there is a higher essence within all objects which is unknown. This essence is what sustains the very atoms which go to make up the objects. But what sustains the atoms? They are not self-sustaining. They come into and out of existence in accordance with a certain plan. Modern physics understands this much. Matter is not "solid" and does not have permanent existence. Energy, mass and time are all relative. These teachings were already understood in Ancient Egypt thousands of years before the development of quantum physics in modern times. The existence of matter and the plan by which it manifests is the work of Ra. This is the higher reality which Aset wanted to know.

Knowing is of two types. Something can be known intellectually. You can have vast knowledge about a subject such as scriptural writings, medical science, etc. However, this knowledge is only useful in the relative world. Mystical knowledge means understanding the very essence of existence. This knowledge transforms the knower. The knower of this kind of knowledge becomes one with the higher essence itself. Therefore, Aset was seeking to transform herself into a higher form of consciousness. So she looked up to the gods and goddesses, but even more so to the spirits, because even the gods and goddesses do not know the absolute name of Ra. Anything that is in a relative form of existence cannot know that which is absolute because the absolute is the totality and a piece cannot know the whole. All of the planes of existence are relative. There are three major planes of existence. Human life occurs in the Physical Plane. The realm of the gods and goddesses is the Astral Plane and the realm of the spirits is the Causal Plane. Beyond the Causal Plane lies the Absolute which transcends all planes. This is where the true name of Ra is to be discovered. This was Aset's true goal. For more on the planes of existence see the book *The Hymns of Amun* by Dr. Muata Ashby.

Ra is the relative name of the Supreme Being. It is like a metaphor or descriptive symbol of the Divine for use in the relative world. The Sages of ancient times created such symbols for the purpose of aiding the mind by providing it with an objective form on which to concentrate. The Ancient Egyptian word, *bes* 𓃀𓈖𓋴𓀭, means "visible image of the god or goddess." The Self or God has no particular form or name. However, images are used for spiritual practice since it is easier at first to worship the Divine as an image. It is an image, with name and form, that is used for devotional purposes and is not to be understood as a reality. In order to grow spiritually an aspirant needs to discover the transcendental name (essence) of the Divine, beyond the images. This occurs when the mind evolves in wisdom and spiritual sensitivity. This means gradually becoming one with the Divine. This was Aset's goal. Aset knew that any person who knows their real, divine, name will attain enlightenment. This is what she means when she says, "The person who hath declared his name shall live."

So Aset decided to stop Ra and force him to give her his absolute name. She took a part of his body (spirit) and a part of the physical universe (earth) and made it into the form of a serpent. The mixing of spirit and matter is a metaphor relating to the reunification of the opposite poles which comprise Creation. When there is vibration in matter, the world exists as a duality with opposite poles (positive and negative, attraction and repulsion, etc.). This means that there are pairs of opposites in Creation, and the mind operates within this understanding. The most important form of duality which operates in every unenlightened human being is individuality. A human being who is ignorant of the Divine Name thinks, "I am an individual, separate and distinct from the rest of the world and from God." The duality of the opposites also refers to male-female, up-down, here-there, yes-no, etc. However, before Creation came into existence there were no opposites, because there was no differentiation in matter. There was just a single essence, the Primeval Ocean, until Ra emerged from the ocean and started to cause ripples (vibrations) in it.

The serpent is the perfect instrument to disable the relative form of Ra. The serpent is a metaphor of the goddess and her energy or power to accomplish any and all tasks, even to stop Creation. The serpent is also a metaphor of the internal Life Force within every human being. The mystical art of awakening this power and directing it towards breaking down the obstacles of spiritual evolution (ignorance, anger, hatred, desire, jealousy, frustration) is known as the Science of the Serpent Power or Serpent Power Yoga.

So Aset's serpent bit Ra which debilitated his ability to maintain Creation. His weakness at this point of the story symbolizes the breakdown of relative knowledge. Ra's journey on the barque sustains the practical (time and space) reality. However, the power of spiritual knowledge and meditation (which Aset practiced) enabled her to go beyond the relative (lower) knowledge. The bite of the serpent is a symbol of the power of wisdom and inquiry into the greatest of all questions, "Who am I?" The venomous power of this way of thinking is infallible in disarming the power of nature to delude a human being. Therefore, the study and practice of mystical philosophy, with the proper guidance, is the greatest weapon against illusion, egoism, greed, selfishness, jealousy, passion, desire, etc. These are the enemies of the soul which obstructs it in its quest to discover its unity with the Divine. It is no wonder why the serpent is the primary symbol of the Goddess in Ancient Egypt.

Thus, the relative form of Ra became weak, and his power to maintain Creation was weakened so much so that his face began to be covered over, as the land is covered during the inundation period of the Nile River. This inundation signals the dissolution of matter as it reverts to its undifferentiated state, which existed before Ra emerged from the Primeval Waters.

So Ra could not withstand Aset's probing. Nature was beginning to show its real essence. It was losing its shapes and forms. Ra allowed himself to be discovered. This discovery bestowed the knowledge of the essential nature of the Divine to Aset. This knowledge cannot be transmitted in words or even in thoughts, ideas or concepts. It is transmitted by one way alone, by communing with its source. This attainment of the special name is not a verbalization but an identification of the knower with that which is known. This is why it was transmitted from the heart of Ra to the heart of Aset and not from his mouth to her ears. This is also why it has a transformative effect on the knower.

To know the essential nature of God is to become one with God. Knowing the essential nature of God, the absolute and transcendental aspect of the Divine, means becoming enlightened. Enlightenment means reaching a state of consciousness that is free from all illusion, all relativity and all limitation. It is becoming one with God, who is omnipotent, immortal, eternal and infinite. Therefore, an enlightened Sage is internally one with the Divine even though his or her body may continue to exist in the relative world. Enlightenment or knowing the essential nature of the Divine means knowing that which when known leaves nothing else to be known. This knowledge is the source of all knowledge and the truth behind all relative truths of the world and of all human experience.

A spiritual aspirant who practices this teaching, that all existence is essentially made up of the same essence, has the power to reveal the secrets of nature and to remove the illusions of life. Also, for one who has discovered the essence of nature, it ceases to exist as such and only the higher nature remains. There is no going back to the state of ignorance once the veil of nature has been lifted. Discovering God's true nature means seeing God everywhere and in all things. Through the process of practicing this spiritual teaching, a person's Serpent Power (Life Force Energy) is aroused. This power disables the illusoriness of the world and the negativity of one's own ego. Negativity and egoism drives people to hold on to the illusions of the world which prevents them from discovering the true essence of the Divine. The Serpent Power Energy allows a person's consciousness to go beyond the illusoriness of the world, carrying it to unite with the very source of consciousness beyond thoughts, individuality and the ego itself.

The poisoning of the relative aspect of Ra is a metaphor relating to the poisoning of an illusion. The relative form of Ra in time and space is an illusion because it is only a reflection of the Absolute. Therefore, the uniting of one's own mind with the Cosmic Mind (The Self-God), meaning the movement away from dualistic thinking and moving closer to the understanding of the oneness which underlies all Creation allows the mind to poison or undermine (sabotage) the power of the illusion of the world. The illusion of dualistic and ignorant thinking is that God has a particular form and that everything in Creation is separate from everything else. Just as waves in the ocean are all rooted in one ocean, and just as your mental thoughts are rooted in your single mind, every object in this universe is rooted in one sustaining essence.

A spiritual aspirant must learn to see the world and the ego as illusions. Then he or she will be in a position to discover their dreamlike quality. The more a person affirms that the ego is real and that it can be satisfied by acquiring wealth and fulfillment of egoistic desires and pleasures, the more its effects appear real to the mind. However, no matter how intense a person's ego becomes, or how wealthy, famous or powerful a person becomes, death is always looming in the shadows. This in itself points to the illusoriness of the ego. That which is finite cannot be real. Therefore, the ego and the world are like the personality we become when having a dream. The world we experience when awake is like the world we experience when asleep and having a dream. They are both illusory. A spiritual aspirant must learn to develop such a powerful intellect that he / she will be able to peer through the illusoriness of the concepts and beliefs of the mind. This movement is what ultimately leads to spiritual enlightenment.

Aset was able to realize (experience) the highest truth by practicing the disciplines of Yoga. Through the power of the Yoga of Wisdom, which relates to acquiring spiritual (intuitional) knowledge and right thinking, she realized that she could attain the higher level of consciousness if she could discover the higher essence of Ra. Aset also developed the power of dispassion and detachment from the world which allowed her to turn away from human life and from the Astral Plane of the gods and goddesses as well. She was able to realize that she could discover the highest secrets of Creation if she could unite the opposites (Yoga of Tantrism). Through her devotion to truth and penetrating inquiry (Yoga of Wisdom and Meditation) into Ra's essential nature she was able to direct all of her attention towards the Divine and pierce the *veil of illusion* (the outer form of an object).

Even though Ra gave her an answer the first time she asked for his name, Aset knew that this was only the temporal (relative) name. Her attainment in wisdom and her higher intuition allowed her to know that what he said was not the higher teaching she wanted. Ra stated that he was the Creator of the gods at the two horizons, meaning all that exists within Creation including the gods and goddesses. Therefore, even the knowledge of the gods and goddesses is lower knowledge of time and space. Ra has three forms. He is the morning sun, the creator of the day. He is the noon day sun, the sustainer of the day. He is also the evening sun or the dissolution of the day. These descriptions refer to the twenty four hour cycle of each day, but in a broader sense they also refer to human life and to Creation itself. Ra sustains an individual's life from birth, to adulthood, and then to death. He also is the cause of the universe coming into existence from the undifferentiated Primeval Ocean which is formless, boundless and infinite, its sustenance over a period of billions of years and its ultimate dissolution back into the undifferentiated Primeval Ocean. These three states of life and Creation are relative because they are conditioned by time and circumstance. What is the nature of the entity who sustains those states but is not affected by them or changed in any way, who is the same in the beginning, middle and end? This is the question which Aset was seeking to answer.

Even though one of Ra's years are like one hundred and twenty five human years in the realm of time and space, what is that as compared to eternity? Eternity and infinity were Aset's real goal and not relativity and the temporal nature of Creation. Aset was after that which is absolute, and not that which is perishable and fleeting. Even a billion years is an infinitesimal speck as compared to eternity. Many spiritual aspirants and the masses of people accept the exoteric teaching of a philosophy as the highest truth, but there is an esoteric philosophy behind the myth. This esoteric or inner teaching is the higher teaching meant for those who are ready to realize the higher truth. It is possible to attain a level of consciousness within which one can exist for a period equal to Ra's life-span, but even this is ultimately perishable, fleeting and illusory.

So when people seek immortality in the realm of time and space or believe that their religion or knowledge is the "real" one or that their picture of God is the "real" one, they are engaging in nothing but ignorance. They are chasing after an illusion. The various forms of the Divine presented in all religions are nothing but symbols. Religious philosophy is only a concept to help an individual turn his/her mind towards the Divine. Symbols and religions are concepts to assist the mind, leading it to discover the higher, transcendental reality. However, those who are un-initiated into the higher teaching and accept the myth on faith will be limited in their spiritual attainment. They will be prone to egoism and erroneous thinking based on the limited powers of their minds and lower desires. They will be susceptible to the greed, animosity, anger, jealousy and hatred of the lower self and thus, they will always be in conflict with themselves and with others. They will repudiate the myths and spiritual philosophy of others and see themselves as the followers of the truth.

An advancing spiritual aspirant, someone who has begun to unite the opposites, begins to see beyond the exoteric form of all religions. He or she begins to understand that the true object of devotion in all religions is the same Supreme Being in its absolute essence. No matter what part of the universe the religion may come from, it is the same Divinity which is being sought through the myths and symbols which are based on specific cultures and traditions. Therefore, the enlightened Sage sees no contradiction in any religion or in any form of worship as long as it is moving towards the realization of the transcendental Self. All forms of worship which fall short of this will be limited.

So Ra agrees to allow himself to be searched and discovered. Aset then assumes all of his power and glory. This is the possibility for all who seek to discover the Divine. This act of assuming the higher personality is in reality the act of becoming who you really are. It means breaking the identification you have with your relative lower self and discovering your transcendental Higher Self (Heru). This is the act of becoming an enlightened personality.

Becoming an enlightened personality does not mean that the practical world comes to an end. This is why Aset, though having come into the knowledge of Ra and having assumed equal power, cures him and allows him to continue sustaining the practical, relative reality. In the same manner, a Sage, though internally experiencing the higher reality, continues to live and exist in the practical reality, assisting others in making their practical life easier so that they may have the opportunity to practice the teachings which lead to spiritual evolution. The difference between an ordinary person and an enlightened Sage is that the Sage is never bound to the world, human emotions or the negative aspects of the mind (anger, frustration, hatred, greed, jealousy, etc.). He or she is always fulfilled, enjoying bliss and inner peace, no matter what may be occurring in the environment. A Sage is always in tune with nature. A Sage is always aware of his or her higher identity. He / she no longer identifies with the limited human ego, mind and body, and therefore is not susceptible to depression or elation of any kind. A Sage sees the ego, the mind and body as tools to carry out the divine work of the Creator, to guide souls to attain spiritual enlightenment.

Aset gains the power to bestow upon her son, Heru, the divine vision which is represented by the eyes of Ra. In this teaching the left eye, the moon, symbolizes intellect or the relative knowledge of the Creation. The right eye represents the essence of the spirit. Both constitute a complementary whole of spiritual consciousness, spiritual enlightenment. This will help him succeed in the struggle to bring justice, truth and righteousness to the world. This is the ideal for all human beings who follow the Goddess. They should see themselves as children of the Goddess. As they put themselves in her care by practicing the teachings of Yoga which she demonstrates through her myth and the disciplines of her temple, they will receive the fruits of spiritual wisdom, divine vision, immortality, and self-discovery or oneness with the Divine.

Thus, Aset is the healer of the greatest illness in all Creation. She heals human beings from the illness of ignorance of their true Self. She is the transmitter of the grace of the Divine to all Creation in the form of the eye of intuitional vision and in the form of her son Heru. Also, she is in possession of the power to assist every human being to survive the poison of ignorance and illusion about the world and about the nature of the Divine Self. This is what Aset meant when she referred to "a certain man, the son of a certain man," i.e., Asar (Osiris) and Heru (Horus), respectively. All spiritual aspirants are Asar and Heru. In the myth of the Ausarian Resurrection Aset resurrects both Heru and Asar through the power which comes from knowing the Divine Name of Ra.

The goal of spiritual enlightenment based on the Story of Ra and Aset may be summarized as follows.

Worldly Knowledge

A spiritual aspirant needs to become self-sufficient and capable of controlling his or her practical life. This means that a person should seek to learn the practical knowledge which will help them to survive in the practical world. Having done this the aspirant needs to always remember that worldly knowledge is lower knowledge. It is used to sustain the practical reality.

Aspiration

Aspiration is the awakening of the Spiritual Self, that is, becoming conscious of the divine presence within one's self and the universe by having faith that there is a spiritual essence beyond ordinary human understanding. It implies a desire to engage in spiritual study and self-discovery. Aspiration also means seeking after spiritual truth through the various disciplines known as Yoga.

Studying and Applying the Wisdom Teachings

Goddess Worship and Rituals of Enlightenment

Studying and applying the wisdom teachings implies practicing the teachings in day to day life. It means seeing beyond the opposites and understanding the underlying essence of Creation.

Inquiry Into Who Am I?

There is no more powerful question which a spiritual aspirant can ask other than "Who am I?" Everything in life depends on one's ego but if you ask the question, "Who am I?" it becomes clearer and clearer that the ego is not the real you, and everything that the ego wants is illusory. This spiritual discipline or practice allows a spiritual aspirant to gradually free himself or herself from the snare of egoism and ignorance.

Single-minded Determination To Know The Highest Truth

A spiritual aspirant cannot be satisfied with the intellectual understanding of "Who am I?" or nature of the Divine. There must be an overwhelming and one-pointed movement towards the ultimate goal, to experience the Divine.

Communion With The Divine

Aset was able to commune with Ra. This is how she obtained his real name. So too a spiritual aspirant must seek to commune with the Divine Self in order to attain enlightenment. This is accomplished by practicing all of the disciplines outlined here and through these, leading oneself into a transcendental state of consciousness which allows one to go beyond the ego and converse intimately with God. This is the ultimate goal which leads a person to become one with God.

Mysticism of the Ancient Egyptian Goddess

A SUMMARY OF THE MYSTICAL SYMBOLISM OF
THE STORY OF
ASAR, ASET AND HERU

Asar represents the human soul which has incarnated on earth in human form. Thus, he represents the innermost reality of all human beings. Life and the physical human existence fall in love with the soul which is symbolized by Nebthet's (Nepthys') love for Asar. Nebthet represents physical pleasure. When the soul forgets its true nature, it becomes overpowered by the lower nature, the ego, as symbolized by Set.

Therefore, Asar's brother, Set, symbolizes egoism and all of the negative qualities which a human being can develop when they are ignorant of their higher essence. The story symbolically relates how the unbridled negative emotions and desires of a human being (the ego), essentially hacks the soul to pieces and attempts to stop any chance for it to reincarnate in order to seek redemption and enlightenment. Set also represents the treachery of the world, that which seems to be a promise of pleasure, but is in reality a snare which enslaves the soul to the myriad forms of misery of human existence. Set represents the distractions and pressure of life to indulge in the pleasures of the senses. Thus, Heru represents spiritual aspiration, the desire to study and practice the teachings and the inner spiritual strength which is required to sublimate the ego and to succeed in the struggle of life.

Aset is the wisdom which allows a person to put together the understanding of their higher reality, the Spirit. She is also the knowledge of how to call to the Divine in order to discover one's spiritual essence. She, together with the inner spirit, as symbolized by the spirit of Asar, is also the power within the heart which gives a person encouragement and strength to face the adversities of the world and then to call out to the Divine in order to attain enlightenment. So when a desire to learn spirituality emerges, it is the spirit of Asar which is urging the aspirant onward. Then that movement towards spirituality is nurtured by the goddess as a mother who brings forth new life and nourishes it to health and growth by protecting it from the elements and from all negative influences until it is strong enough to stand on its own. Apuat represents the development of intellectual discrimination, the ability to understand truth from untruth, reality from unreality, and Sebek represents the power of the lower nature, the physical body, when it is sublimated and placed in the service of the Higher Self.

For a more detailed study of the Ausarian Resurrection Myth it is highly recommended that you review the books, "The Ausarian Resurrection: The Ancient Egyptian Bible" and "The Mystical Teachings of the Ausarian Resurrection: Initiation Into The Third Level of Shetaut Asar" by Dr. Muata Ashby.

56

PART III The Forms of The Goddess and Introduction to Teachings of The Temple of Aset (Isis)

In order to discover or unveil the goddess and her teachings, we will need to explore her many forms. It is important to understand that all of the forms of the Goddess are symbolic representations of the one Supreme Being. The most popular form of the Goddess in Ancient Egypt throughout all its periods was Aset. Aset and her husband Asar were worshipped throughout the ancient world even though they were indigenous Egyptian deities, dating back to prehistoric times (before 5,000 B.C.E.). In the first century B.C. E. Aset was one of the most popular goddesses in the city of Rome. Her temples in Rome were filled with altars, statues, obelisks, etc., brought from Egypt, and orders of priestesses were endowed in order to perform the "Mysteries of Aset" and other Egyptian miracle plays in the great temples of the city. From Rome, the cult of Isis spread to Spain, Portugal, Gey, Gaul, Switzerland, Marseilles, and to North Africa. In a manner similar to which Aset was identified with many other goddesses in Egypt and Nubia, in foreign lands other goddesses were given her attributes. Some of the foreign goddesses were Selene, Demeter or Ceres, Aphrodite, Venus, Proserpine, Juno, Nemesis, Fortuna, anthea, etc.

In the *Golden Ass* of Apuleius of Madura, Isis says to Lucius:

"The whole earth worships my godhead, one and individual, under many a changing shape, with varied rites, and by many diverse names. There the Phrygians, first-born of men, call me "mother of the gods that dwell in Pessinus;" there the Athenians, sprung from the soil they till, know me the Rhamnusian, but those on whom shine the first rays of the Sun-god as each day he springs to new birth, the Arii and the Ethiopians and the Egyptians, mighty in ancient lore, honour me with my peculiar rites, and call me by my true name of *'Isis (Aset), the Queen'*."

From here we will begin to explore the many forms of the Goddess and their symbolic-mystical importance. Symbols are the most important form in which the mind communicates. Everything that you think about, the ideas, the thoughts, are all in symbolic form in your mind. (For more on the subject see *Egyptian Yoga: The Philosophy of Enlightenment*). Mystical symbols are a form of mystical language which express teachings that affect the mind in an unconscious way so as to instill an understanding of mystical reality, and in so doing, awaken deep impressions of the true Self.

In ancient times the Goddess was depicted in many forms which utilized many attributes of various animals. These included the bird, the hippopotamus, the cow, the lion, the vulture, and the cat. The use of the animal reference is a symbolic allusion to the teaching associated with the particular depiction. So the wings are used, they symbolize the ability to

57

soar high above all and to encompass all. If the cow is used, it symbolizes the burgeoning Life Force energy which nurtures all, and so on.

Nathor
The Winged Nile Goddess

We will begin with one of the earliest known forms of the Ancient Egyptian Goddess. She is popularly known as *Nathor*, the winged Nile Goddess. Nathor is a pre-dynastic (before 5,000 B.C.E.) depiction of the Goddess. The striking features she displays are her wings. From ancient times, wings symbolize the all encompassing nature of the Supreme Being. Thus the Goddess at once symbolizes the all encompassing mother, who gives birth to the universe and enfolds it in her arms.

From ancient times the Goddess has been the symbol of nature and God has been the symbol of the spirit. Why should this be so? Think of Creation. Like human existence it expresses in opposites, male and female. Nature is the life sustaining and nurturing force while the essence of life dwells within it, grows and expands. This is why nature is likened to the female, and particularly to a mother who nurses her young. The mother is the protector and nurse. The male figure brings to mind images of guidance and discipline, which ideas have been associated with the male (God) forms of the Divine.

As you will see shortly, the principle of the spirit (God) within Creation (Goddess) became an important teaching which was expressed in the Ancient Egyptian teaching in reference to Hetheru and Heru. Also, in the form of Maat, the Goddess symbolizes the very foundation upon which Creation and everything in Creation has been based as the protector and sustainer and the embodiment of truth, order and justice.

Goddess Worship and Rituals of Enlightenment

The Goddess of Creation

Goddess Mehurt

An Ancient Egyptian Creation myth holds that all came into existence out of a Primeval Ocean of unformed matter, the Duat (Duat). The teaching of the fullness of the Primeval Ocean is to be found in the *Book of Coming Forth By Day* (xvii. 76,79; lxxi. 13; cxxiv. 17). The hekau-utterance in Chapter xvii gives an exact description of the concept of "fullness" and of the female nature of the Primeval Ocean. The initiate says:

"Behold Ra who was born yesterday from the buttocks of the Goddess Mehurt." In the answer to the question: "What then is this?," it is explained: "It is the watery abyss of heaven, or as others say, It is the image of the Eye of Ra in the morning at His daily birth. Mehurt is the Eye (Utchat) of Ra."

The seven Hetheru Cow Goddesses and the Bull Asar

Mehurt was originally the female embodiment of the watery matter, the Primeval Ocean from which the substance of the world was formed and from which Ra emerged. In other versions of the Creation story, the Primeval Ocean is referred to as Nu, a male form. Thus, the Primeval Ocean is seen as an *androgynous* essence from which all arose in the form of opposites. Mehurt, ⟨hieroglyphs⟩, means **"mighty fullness."** She symbolizes the infinite source of matter which is impregnated by the male spirit. This is one of the reasons why one of the symbols of Amun (Ancient Egyptian name for God-Supreme Being) is a pregnant woman ⟨hieroglyph⟩ . Of course, the female primeval matter and the male spirit are both aspects of the same energy. This is expressed in the last line of the utterance where it is explained that Mehurt herself is the "image" of the "Eye of Ra." The Eye of Ra is his own daughter, Hetheru. Mehurt is depicted as a cow Goddess brimming with life giving essence. The symbol of the cow is also common to Hetheru, Nut and

Mysticism of the Ancient Egyptian Goddess

Aset. The Goddess in the form of a cow is often referred to as a "seven fold deity" known as the "seven Hetherus" who preside over the life of each individual and the course of Creation. This title refers to the further differentiation of the three primordial principles of the Trinity (Asar-Aset-Heru) which is expressed as the phenomenal universe through a series of sevens. This number, *seven*, is expressed in all levels of Creation. It is expressed in the seven levels of the human subtle anatomy with the seven spiritual centers (see *Egyptian Yoga: The Philosophy of Enlightenment* and *The Serpent Power*), and also as the seven primary colors of the rainbow. This principle of sevens translated into the Gnostic idea of the "seven planetary spirits," and the Christian Archangels, known as the *Heads of the Celestial Host*, were titled the "Seven Archangels of the Presence." Seven is also a special number to the Ancient Egyptian goddess Sesheta.

Aset-Hetheru in Ancient Egypt symbolized the source of Creation. The *Milky Way* was produced by her udder. She was "the Great Cow which gave birth to Ra, the Great Goddess, the mother of all the gods and goddesses...the lady who existed when nothing else had being, and who created that which came into being." The cow is therefore a prominent representation of Aset and Hetheru. In her form as seven cows, Hetheru, an aspect of Aset, symbolizes the seven energies which course through the universe and which are engendered by the *Bull* (Osiris-male aspect of the Supreme Being). The *Bull* is a metaphor for the spirit. Just as the bull on a farm sires many cows, so to the "Bull" (Supreme Spirit) engenders all life in Creation.

In Indian Mythology, the cow holds a similar symbolism as that of Ancient Egypt. The cow is known as the "fountain of milk and curds." In a mystical sense, the world is a curd of the milk which emanated from the Celestial Cow (Goddess).

Nut as the Cow Goddess
(The Cosmic Mother of Creation)

Nut, Shu, Geb and Ra in his boat

The Celestial Cow is one of the primary forms of the goddess Nut. Nut is the daughter of Shu and Tefnut who are themselves children of Ra, the transcendental Self. Her body is the heavens and embedded in it are the stars in the sky. Thus she is the womb of Creation or it might be said that Creation is within her. The earth hangs in space which is her body. One version of the Creation story tells how Ra traverses in his barque over Nut's back, and every evening she consumes him and every morning she gives birth to him as the morning sun. (see *The Ausarian Resurrection*).

Forms of Aset (Isis)
Love, Cosmic Consciousness and Wisdom.

In the temple of Denderah, it is inscribed that Nut gave birth to Isis there, and that upon her birth, Nut exclaimed: "Ås (behold), *I have become thy mother.*" This was the origin of the name "Åst," or Aset. The Greeks and others knew her later as Isis. The

61

Mysticism of the Ancient Egyptian Goddess

text further states that she was a dark-skinned child and was called *"Khnemet-ankhet"* or the lady of love. Likewise, Hetheru is also of dark complexion. Thus, like Asar, Aset also symbolizes the "blackness" of the vast unmanifest regions of existence, or the immense region of the unconscious mind. This identification is also symbolized in her aspect as *Amentet,* or the Duat, itself. Therefore, Amentet (Aset) and the soul of Amentet (Asar) are in reality one and the same. In her aspect as Amentet, Aset represents the subtle substance of nature, the astral plane.

In the epic saga of *The Ausarian Resurrection,* the love of Aset was instrumental in discovering and putting the pieces of Asar's dead body back together. The two most important attributes which Isis encompasses are love and wisdom. Aset's undying love and devotion to Asar enabled her to revive him. And again, after Asar was torn apart by his evil brother, Set this divine devotion led her to discover the pieces of Asar' dead body. Her love also caused the resurrection of her son, Horus, as well. This is a reference to the devotion that the spiritual aspirant must have in order to lead him or her to reconstruct his or her own divine being. In this aspect Aset is that a deep, ardent love and devotion for the Divine are the keys to divine realization.

In her name, *Rekhat,* Aset is *"the Lady of Wisdom"* or the embodiment of wisdom, and also represents *rekhit* or wisdom. She is the patroness of all *rekht* or Sages. Aset represents the kind of wisdom which transcends all intellectual knowledge. She is at the same time the ultimate reality (Amentet) behind Creation as well as the *Rekh* (knowledge and understanding) of that Creation. Thus, it is said that she veils herself and that "no man has unveiled her." The wisdom of Creation or knowing Aset in her full essence means becoming one with her in consciousness. When this unity occurs, one transcends ordinary human consciousness, so in this sense, no worldly human can discover her. The wisdom of Aset refers to that profound understanding of the essence of the Divine which is devoid of any kind of ignorance or illusion in reference to the transcendental Self. This wisdom is the intuitional realization which comes from pondering the nature of the Divine and it transcends scholarly knowledge. Pondering implies repeated reflection and meditation on the Divine, trying with sincerity and humility, to understand and become one with the Divine by discovering a deeper basis to one's personality.

Aset is also a healer. She healed the body of Asar even after it had been dismembered into several pieces. As the Goddess, she assists all those who pray to her, bestowing health and well being. She manifests in the form of love, a mother's love, valor, devotion to God and intuitional realization of the Higher Self, Enlightenment. In yoga philosophy "true health" is termed "being established in the Self" (the state of Enlightenment). Although you need to have a healthy diet, proper exercise and rest to maintain health, these factors alone can never confer total health. You must engage in spiritual practices to discover your true nature to be truly healthy. This was one of the most important teachings given in the Ancient Egyptian Temple of Aset.

Forms of Hetheru
(Hathor)
Spiritual Power and Sexual Energy

In a text from the Temple at Dier al-Medina, Hetheru is referred to as having the same divine attributes as Horus. She is described as *The Golden One* and *The Queen of the Gods.* Her shrines are even more numerous than those of Horus. Hetheru or *Het-Heru,* meaning *The House of Horus* and *The House Above* (heavens), became identified, like Horus, with the salvation of the initiate. In the *Egyptian Book of Coming*

Forth By Day, she is the one who urges the initiate to do battle with the monster Apep (symbol of egoism which spurs negativity and evil) so as not to lose his / her heart as she cries out: *"Take your armor."* In a separate papyrus, the initiate is told that she (Hetheru) is the one who: *"will make your face perfect among the Gods; she will open your eye so that you may see every day... she will make your legs able to walk with ease in the Underworld, Her name is Hetheru, Lady of Amenta."*

In Chapter 81- utterance 1, the role of Hetheru in the process of salvation is specified as the initiate speaks the words which will help him / her become as a lotus:

"I am the lotus pure coming forth from the god of light, the guardian of the nostril of Ra, the guardian of the nose of Hetheru; I make my journey; I run after him who is Horus. I am the pure one coming forth from the field."

The lotus has been used since ancient times to symbolize the detachment and dispassion that a spiritual aspirant must develop. The lotus emerges everyday out of the murky waters of the pond in order to receive the rays of the sun. The spiritual aspirant, a follower of the Goddess, must rise above egoism and negativity (anger, hatred, greed, ignorance) in life in order to perceive the light of wisdom and attain spiritual enlightenment. Hetheru and Horus form a composite archetype, a savior with all of the complementary qualities of the male and female principles, inseparable, complete and androgynous.

Hetheru represents the power of Ra, the Supreme Spirit, therefore, associating with her implies coming into contact with the boundless source of energy which sustains the universe. Therefore, making contact with Hetheru implies developing inner will-power which engenders clarity of vision that will lead to the discovery of what is righteous and what is unrighteous. A mind which is constantly distracted and beset with fetters (anger, hatred, greed, conceit, covetousness, lust, selfishness, etc.) cannot discern the optimal course in life. It becomes weak willed because the negative emotions and feelings drain the mental energy. Thus unrighteous actions and sinful thoughts arise and the weak mind cannot resist them. Unrighteous actions lead to adverse situations and adverse situations lead to pain and sorrow in life. (see *The Ausarian Resurrection* and *Egyptian Tantra Yoga* for more on Hetheru and the teachings of Egyptian Tantra Yoga)

Forms of Maat
Order, Righteousness, Justice,
Balance, Harmony, Truth

"Those who live today will die tomorrow,
those who die tomorrow will be born again;
Those who live MAAT will not die."

When Ra emerged in his Barque for the first time and Creation came into being, he was standing on the pedestal of Maat. Thus the Creator, Ra, lives by Maat and has established Creation on Maat. Who is Maat? Maat is the form of the Goddess who represents the very order which constitutes Creation. Therefore, it is said that Ra created the universe by putting Maat in the place of chaos. So Creation itself is Maat. Creation without order is chaos. Maat is a profound teaching in reference to the nature of Creation and the manner in which human conduct should be cultivated. It refers to a deep understanding of Divinity and the manner in which virtuous qualities can be developed in the human heart so as to come closer to the Divine.

Maat is a philosophy, a spiritual symbol as well as a cosmic energy or force which pervades the entire universe. She is the symbolic embodiment of world order, justice, righteousness, correctness, harmony and peace. She is also known by her headdress composed of a feather of truth. She, as a form of the Goddess Aset, represents living a life of righteous action, orderly life which lead to balance and equanimity of mind. Balance and equanimity of mind lead to wisdom and spiritual awakening because when the mind is calmed the underlying divine essence can then be discovered.

65

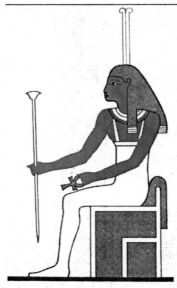

Goddess Meskhent

In Ancient Egypt, the judges and all those connected with the judicial system were initiated into the teachings of Maat. Thus, those who would discharge the laws and regulations of society were well trained in the ethical and spiritual values of life, fairness, justice and the responsibility to serve society in order to promote harmony in society and the possibility for spiritual development in an atmosphere of freedom and peace. For only when there is justice and fairness in society can there be abiding harmony and peace. Harmony and peace are necessary for the pursuit of true happiness and inner fulfillment in life.

Meskhent and Renennet

Goddess Worship and Rituals of Enlightenment

Along with her associates, the *Shai* (fate or destiny-sometimes refered to as husband of Rennenet), *Rennenet* (fortune) and *Meskhenet*, Maat encompasses the teachings of Karma and Reincarnation or the destiny of every individual based on past actions, thoughts and feelings. Thus, they have an important role to play in the Judgment scene of the *Book of Coming Forth By Day*. Understanding their principles leads the aspirant to become free of the cycle of reincarnation and human suffering and to discover supreme bliss and immortality. If a person is ignorant about their higher essential nature, they will only have knowledge of human existence. At the time of death their soul will wander and experience either heavenly or hellish conditions, in much the same way as you experience good and bad dreams. Spiritual enlightenment means discovering your essential nature as one with the Supreme Self, and when this is achieved, there is no more hell or heaven; there is a resurrection in consciousness. This is what the Goddess urges every aspirant to achieve through study, reflection and meditation on her teachings, and it is the central theme in the *Ausarian Resurrection* myth. (see the Book *The Wisdom of Maati* for more on Maat philosophy.)

Sefkhet-aabut
(Sesheta, Sheshat, Seseshat)

The goddess Seshat is the female counterpart of Djehuti and an aspect of Maat-Aset. She is the goddess of learning, construction and letters. She is associated with Rennenet. Sesheta means the goddess of the seven. Thus, she presides over the teachings which relate to the seven realms of Creation. In this way she is related to the seven Hetherus who are supported by the Divine Bull of Ament (Asar). She wears a panther skin garment symbolizing that she has conquered the lower nature.

Mysticism of the Ancient Egyptian Goddess

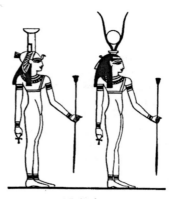

Nebt-het
(Nephthys)
Nature, Worldly Consciousness and Death.

In the Ausarian Resurrection, Nebthet is the sister of Asar and Aset and the consort of Set. She represents the gross aspect of nature and the natural phase of life called decay and death. Nature is what the spirit impregnates with its life giving essence. According to natural law, anything that is born must be subject to the laws of nature and ultimately die. In the epic story of *The Ausarian Resurrection,* Asar' original form was detached from nature. Asar was timeless, immortal, and untouched by the passions and frailties of human nature as the spirit of Ra. As an incarnation of the Divine (Ra), Asar become intoxicated with nature, his own Creation, and became associated with it through intercourse with Nebthet. Asar, as a symbol of the human soul, is a stark example of the fate of human existence. His situation embodies the predicament of every individual human being. This is why the Ancient Egyptian Pharaohs and all initiated into the mystery of Asar are referred to as Asar and or Heru, and are considered to be the husband, or daughter or son, respectively, of Aset. Just as Asar became intoxicated with his own Creation, so too the human soul becomes involved with nature and thereby produces a physical body composed of an aggregate of gross physical elements (water, earth, fire, air). The union between Asar (Soul-Divine Self) and Nebthet (physical-gross nature) begets Apuat (Anpu), who represents spiritual aspiration and devotion. When the soul evolves it communes with higher nature in the form of Aset. The union between Asar (the Soul) and Aset (Wisdom-subtle nature) begets Horus, the Higher Self (Enlightenment). Therefore, nature (Aset and Nebthet) is the recipient of Asar's seed (spirit).

There is deep mystical symbolism in the images and teachings surrounding the Triad of Asar, Aset and Nebthet. In the temples of *Denderah, Edfu* and *Philae,* there are sculptured representations of the Mysteries of Asar. These show *The Asar* (initiate) lying on a bier (ritual bed), and Aset and Nebthet, who stand nearby, being referred to as the "two widows" of the dead Asar. These images form the basis of the *Ushet Rekhat Ritual.* Aset and Nebthet are depicted as looking exactly alike, the only difference being in their headdresses: Aset 𓊨, Nebthet 𓎼 or 𓎽. However, the symbols of these goddesses are in reality just inverted images of each other. The symbol of Aset is the symbol of Nebthet, when inverted 𝕁➔🯅. Therefore, each is a reflection of the other. Thus, it can be said that both life and death are aspects of the same principle.

The bodies and facial features of Aset and Nebthet are exactly alike. This likeness which Aset and Nebthet share is important when they are related to Asar. As Asar sits on the throne (see page 23), he is supported by the two goddesses, Aset and Nebthet. Symbolically, Asar represents the Supreme Soul, the all-encompassing Divinity which transcends time and space. Aset represents wisdom and enlightened consciousness. She is the knower of all words of power and has the power to resurrect Asar and Horus. Nebthet represents temporal consciousness or awareness of time and space. She is related to mortal life and mortal death. Thus, the state of spiritual Enlightenment is being referred to here as Aset, and it is this enlightened state of mind which the initiate in the Ausarian Mysteries (*Asar Shetaiu*) has as the goal. The Enlightenment of Asar is the state of consciousness in which one is aware of the transient aspects of Creation (Nebthet) as well as the transcendental (Aset). Aset represents the transcendental aspect of matter, that is, matter when seen through the eyes of wisdom rather than through the illusions produced by the ego which can only see Nebthet (gross nature and temporal existence). So, an enlightened personality is endowed with dual consciousness. To become one with Asar means to attain the consciousness of Asar, to become aware of the transcendental, infinite and immortal nature (Aset) while also being aware of the temporal and fleeting human nature (Nebthet).

In the *Book of the Dead* (Chap. xvii. 30), the initiate (spiritual aspirant) identifies with Amsu-Min as part of the ritual and says:

> *"I am the god Amsu (Min) in his coming forth; may his two plumes be set upon my head for me."* In answer to the question, *" Who then is this?"* the text goes on to say, *"Amsu is Heru, **the avenger of his father**, and his coming forth is his birth. The plumes upon his head are Aset and Nebthet when they go forth to set themselves there, even as his protectors, and they provide that which his head lacketh, or (as others say), they are the two exceedingly great uraei which are upon the head of their father **Tem**, or (as others say), his two eyes are the two plumes which are upon his head."*

The passage above provides an exact idea about the true nature of Aset and Nebthet. They are complementary goddess principles which operate to manifest life-death-life or the cycle of birth-death-rebirth known as reincarnation (Nebthet) and that state of consciousness which transcends the cycle of birth and death (Aset). Aset and Nebthet are also known as *Rekhtti: The Two Goddesses*. They also manifest in the Judgment hall of Maat in the *Egyptian Book of Coming Forth By Day* as *Maati* or the double Maat goddesses who watch over the weighing of the heart of the initiate in their name as *Rekhtti Merti neb-ti Maati*. Aset and Nebthet are the basis of the judgment of the soul and the criterion which decides its fate in life as well as after death.

An important teaching presented here is that Aset and Nebthet are identified as the Arati or "the two exceedingly great uraei." They are the two forces of the Serpent Power, *Arat* or Uraeus, also known in India as Kundalini. The Serpent Power refers to the Life Force energy which manifests in the physical human body in the form of two opposites. In Ancient Egyptian mythology and yoga, the two opposites are known as "Uatchit (Arat, Wadjet) and Nekhebet" or the goddesses of the North (Lower Egypt) and of the South (Upper Egypt), "The Two Lands," or "Aset and Nebthet" or "The Two Ladies." In India they are known as "Ida and Pingala."

The opposites also refer to the solar pole (male) and the lunar pole (female) or the active and passive nature of the energies, respectively. In reality the energy is one and the same. It originates from the same source but it manifests as opposites due to the polarization it assumes. Thus, it may be seen as male and female. The Serpent Power energy resides at the base of the spine. When aroused through spiritual evolution (practice of yoga), it courses through the body, finally reaching the crown of the head and re-uniting into its original oneness; the poles dissolve, leaving oneness of consciousness or enlightenment. (see the book *The Serpent Power* for more on the Serpent Power)

Amentet
The Hidden Region

Ament means "hidden." It is a specific reference to the female form of the astral plane or Netherworld known as *Amenta* or the Duat (Duat). Aset was known as the dark-skinned daughter of Nut. Like Asar, her husband, who was known as the "Lord of the Perfect Black," Aset was the "Mistress of the Netherworld" known as Amentet (Amentat). Thus, Aset also symbolizes the "blackness" of the vast unmanifest regions of existence (the unmanifest). Her identification is also symbolized in her aspect as *Amentet*, the Duat, itself. So Aset, in the form of Amentet, is the soul of Amenta (Asar). Thus, Asar, Amenta or the realm of Asar, and Aset are in reality one and the same.

Thus, Aset and Asar together form the hidden recesses of Creation. In essence they are the source of Creation and are therefore both simultaneously considered to be the source of the Life Force which courses through Creation.

Nekhebet-Mut
The Vulture

The vulture is a very important symbol of the Goddess. The vulture feeds upon carrion, the dead carcasses of animals which die. It symbolizes regeneration because like nature, it recycles the dead matter and from it brings forth new life. Therefore, the Goddess, as mother nature, is likened to the vulture.

In Shetaut Amun (Ancient Egyptian Theban Mystical Religion) Nekhebet-Mut is the consort of Amun . She is the Creation itself while Amun is the spirit which lives in and enlivens Creation. In association with the vulture as *Mut*, she represents the female power of nature (physical nature is the consort of the spirit) to recycle and regenerate dead matter and bring it back to life. Therefore she is the *Great Mother*. In the Hymns of Amun, verse 41, it is stated: *His (Amun's) wife is the Earth, He united with her.*

Sekhmet-Bast
The Feline Aspect

One important element of the Goddess is the feline aspect. In nature, cats have an inimical relationship with serpents. A special image of the goddess Sekhmet shows her holding the two forces (positive and negative) which together manifest as the opposites of Creation. So in this aspect Sekhmet is likened to the caduceus of Tehuti. She is the consort of the god Ptah and is therefore the dynamic aspect of the spirit (Ptah), the very.life force of Creation. Sekhmet is the central channel while the two serpents symbolize the solar and lunar poles. Note that the two serpents are in reality one serpent with two heads. This signifies that the energy, while appearing as opposites in the form of two serpents (positive and negative), is in reality two aspects of the same energy. When the opposite forces in the mind and body are harmonized there is a dawning of the vision of universality and union which underlies all.

Sekhmet is closely related to the serpent goddess in all her forms of manifestation and therefore she is also a presiding deity of the Serpent Power or internal Life Force energy. In Ancient Egyptian Mystical terminology *Sekhem* is the Life Force energy of Creation. This word is contained in *Sekhemet's* name. Also, she is related to the *skhem* or sistrum. Therefore, she is the goddess of the Life Force.

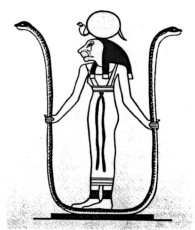

Goddess Sekhmit holding the Serpents of the Life Force

In Ancient Egyptian mythology, the *Serpent of Darkness* is seen as the embodiment of ignorance and evil which threatens the movement of the Barque of Ra and which prevents the spiritual aspirant from attaining enlightenment. Therefore, the Goddess in the form of a cat (Bast), lioness (Sekhmet) or lynx (Hetheru) is seen as the warrior and champion of the gods (Asar and Heru) as well as the aspirant. She is the one who paves the way for spiritual evolution by destroying the evil of ignorance and sinfulness in the human heart.

The god Djehuti holding the Caduceus

Goddess Worship and Rituals of Enlightenment

Sekhmet-Bast-Ra
The All - Goddess

Another important form of the Goddess is known as *Sekhmet-Bast-Ra*. Sekhmet-Bast-Ra is a composite depiction of the Goddess encompassing all of the attributes of the goddesses as well as the attributes of the gods. This is a recognition that all things in Creation are not absolutely female or male. All of Creation is a combination of male and female elements. Therefore, since Creation is androgynous, so too Divinity and the human soul are also androgynous. This understanding is reflected in the following instruction from Aset to Heru in the Ausarian Resurrection.

"Souls, Heru, son, are of the self same nature in themselves, in that they are from one and the same place where the Creator modeled them; nor male nor female are they. Sex is a thing of bodies, not of souls."

Arat (Art, Aart, Arati)
(The Serpent Form of The Goddess)

The Serpent form of the Goddess represents several important teachings related to the Life Force energy (Sekhem) permeating Creation. Emanating from the Divine Self, it enlivens and sustains all of Creation. It also refers to the internal Life Force energy which lies dormant within every human being. This Life Force energy is known in modern times as *Kundalini*.

The symbol of the serpent is used because it is the perfect metaphor to represent the serpentine mode of movement which characterizes the Serpent Power energy. In the teaching of the Temple of Aset from Ancient Egypt the Serpent Power (Arat) was symbolized as the image of a serpent with three and a half coils. Later in history, the same image was used in India to represent the same teaching.

For more on the teachings of the Serpent Power and the spiritual disciplines related to its development for the purpose of promoting spiritual evolution see the book *The Serpent Power* by Dr. Muata Ashby.

Mysticism of the Ancient Egyptian Goddess

The
Goddess
Uadjit

The
Goddess
Nekhebet

Above: The Basket of Aset,
displaying the Serpent Power.

The Egyptian
Serpent Goddess

Uri-hekau,
the Cobra-goddess of
words of power

Right: Arat, The
Serpent Power
also known as
the emblem of
all Goddesses.

THE DIVINE NAMES OF THE GODDESS

Names are very important because they relate to the essence of an object, idea or a person. This means that a name is an essential part of the existence of a thing. Otherwise, without a name it does not exist and conversely without coming into existence it does not receive a name. This is why in Ancient Egyptian mysticism the spirit is regarded as having a name, *Ren*. Everything in time and space receives a name.

The forms of the Goddess are no exception. They receive names which denote the qualities which they exemplify. In this manner the various aspects of the Divine can be explored and understood. The different goddess manifestations are in reality relative manifestations, in time and space, of the Supreme Goddess who is transcendent of time and space. Just as the goddesses emanate from the one Supreme Goddess, this entire universe full of a multiplicity of items, everything seeming to be different from everything else, is in reality an emanation from the one Supreme Self. Thus, the aspects of each goddess are related to the supreme Goddess. Sekhmet-Bast-Ra is a prime example of the figure of the Goddess comprising all gods and goddesses. However, just like every wave is essentially the ocean, every goddess is said to be the "supreme one." Therefore, each one is to be understood as being the representation of the Absolute. This means that the transcendental aspect of each goddess is one and the same. Consequently, any goddess can be worshipped as the Supreme One and the worship of any one of them will lead a spiritual aspirant to discover the transcendental aspect of the Divine if the spiritual practice is entered into with the correct understanding and devotion.

The mind, the power of thinking and rationalizing, is what sustains a human being's notion of existence or non-existence, reality or un-reality. However, consciousness is what sustains the mind just as the ocean sustains the waves. Names are given through the power of speech. Speech is related to the mind or consciousness. It is its mode of manifestation. If the mind speaks worldly knowledge based on ignorance, then the speech and all of the notions and actions it supports will lead a person to ignorance and delusion. If the mind or consciousness is purified, it will allow a person to discover the deeper essence of their own consciousness.

In another Ancient Egyptian myth, Aset acquired the name of Ra, her father (Supreme Being). In doing so she acquired the knowledge which relates to the very essence of existence. This supreme wisdom allows its possessor to have control over nature, life and death, etc. It is this power that she used to resurrect Asar and Heru. In the same manner, the devotees of the Temple of Aset study the names and forms of Aset in order to receive the same knowledge which leads to immortality and abiding happiness. Therefore, the understanding of the names of the goddess allows a person to understand the nature of Creation itself. This understanding bestows expansion in consciousness and spiritual enlightenment.

Mysticism of the Ancient Egyptian Goddess

The ritual of uttering the names of the goddess promotes purity of the speech. This purity was known as *maakheru* in Ancient Egyptian terminology. Maakheru is the primary objective of every spiritual aspirant. The names may be recited, chanted or used in song. The art of recital, chanting and singing the divine names supports the study of the mystical teachings given in the myths related to the various forms of the Goddess. Also, it bestows psychic powers on the aspirant which will allow him or her to achieve great heights of spiritual experience internally and also to perform great works in the world of time and space (human experience).

The Ancient Egyptian Goddess Names:

Apt, Nut, Mehurt, Aset, Hetheru, Maat, Rennenet, Meskhenet, Sefkhet-aabut, Nebthet, Ament, Nekhebet, Mut, Rekhat, Sekhmet, Arat, Bast, Ra, Sekhmet-Bast-Ra.

The Ancient Egyptian Attribute Names:

"The divine one, the only one, the greatest of the gods and goddesses, the queen of all gods, the female Ra, the female Horns, the eye of Ra, the crown of Ra-Heru, Sept, opener of the year, lady of the New Year, maker of the sunrise, lady of heaven, the light-giver of heaven, lady of the North Wind, queen of the earth, most mighty one, queen of the South and North, lady of the solid earth, lady of warmth and fire, benefactress of the Duat, she who is greatly feared in the Duat, the God-mother, the God mother of Heru-ka-nekht, the mother of the Horns of gold, the lady of life, lady of green crops, the green goddess (Uatchet), lady of bread, lady of beer, lady of abundance, lady of joy and gladness, lady of love, the maker of kings, lady of the Great House, lady of the House of fire, the beautiful goddess, the lady of words of power, lady of the shuttle, daughter of Seb, daughter of Neb-er-tcher, the child of Nut, wife of Ra, wife of the lord of the abyss, wife of the lord of the Inundation, the creator of the Nile flood."

THE TEMPLE OF ASET

There is much known about the teachings because of the Ancient Egyptian papyruses which speak about the goddess and her worship as well as the writings of the Greeks who were accepted as initiates into the Temple of Isis and who thereafter began writing about their experiences and the rituals which were carried out. Plutarch was one of the most important writers on the teachings and practices at the Temple of Isis. The teachings include instructions about mystical wisdom, and also references to the practical matters of life such as diet, sex-sublimation and the manner for conducting spiritual studies. They outline what it means to be a spiritual aspirant and the process of mystical evolution.

In the teachings of the Temple of Aset, a devotee of Aset is described as: *One who ponders over sacred matters and seeks therein for hidden truth.* It is not enough to just hear the ancient myths or to understand them at an intellectual level. The aspirant must go deep within him/herself to discover the subtle ideas being conveyed. *Plutarch* describes the character of an initiate of Isis as:

*He alone is a true servant or follower of this goddess who, after has heard, and has been made acquainted in a proper manner (initiated into the philosophy) with the history of the actions of these gods, searches into the hidden truths which lie concealed under them, and examines the whole by the dictates of reason and philosophy. Nor indeed, ought such an examination to be looked on as unnecessary whilst there are so many ignorant of the true reason even of the most ordinary rites observed by the Egyptian priests, such as their shavings and wearing linen garments. Some, indeed, there are, who never trouble themselves to think at all about these matters, whilst others rest satisfied with the most superficial accounts of them: They pay a peculiar veneration to the sheep, therefore they think it their duty not only to abstain from eating flesh, but likewise from wearing its wool. They are continually mourning for their gods, therefore they shave themselves. ***

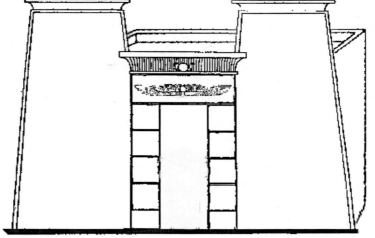

Temple of Aset
Agilkya Island (Egypt, Africa)

Goddess Worship and Rituals of Enlightenment

According to the instructions of the Temple of Aset, a spiritual aspirant needs to engage in the following process of spiritual practice:

1- Listening to the teachings.
2- Constant study and reflection on the teachings along with practicing them in everyday life situations.
3- Meditation on the meanings of the teachings.*

Throughout our journey we have discovered that the Goddess has many names and many forms. Some were based on the particular geographical area of Ancient Egypt which worshipped a particular form of the deity. However, the ancient scriptures clearly show that all the names and images are in reality referring to one and the same Goddess in her many forms. The different names and forms used to describe her and the different situations in which she is described were meant for the purpose of expounding on particular teachings. In fact, just as it can be said that the Supreme Being as a male form created the universe, it can be said that the Supreme Being in the female form created the universe.

*see the book: *The Wisdom of Isis* by Dr, Muata Ashby, for a detailed study of the Teachings of the Temple of Isis.

PART IIII Ushet Rekhat:
The Mother Worship Ritual

INTRODUCTION

Rituals are a powerful process which can lead the mind toward either spiritual thoughts and aspirations or toward pain and sorrow in life. People cling to ignorance by constantly seeking for pleasure and fulfillment in the world of time and space, by seeking human relationships, wealth, possessions, etc. Examples of negative rituals are: overindulgence in recreation, overindulgence in watching television, gossiping, overindulgence in partying and thrill-seeking. In the course of ordinary life you may experience these but if you rely on them as sources of pleasure and happiness you are bound for disappointments. All of life's activities are ritualistic to some degree. Every day we repeat many actions such as eating, sleeping, going to work, school or watching television. Other activities are less frequent but just as ritualistic; these include marriage, childbearing, etc. The basis of society's rituals is custom and habit. Society teaches and socializes young individuals into the activities it deems acceptable and thereby societal rituals develop. Rituals can be bad or good according to the level of spiritual realization within the individual as well as the society as a whole. If a society allows material values to be most important or if the exploitation of some of its members is allowed, then rituals and customs develop which affirm those belief systems. When society developed the materialistic view of life and discounted spiritual values, material values became part of the general culture. Thus, pursuing material wealth and the experience of sensual pleasures have become the most commonly practiced rituals in modern day society. This is reflected in business, government, the media and in the family way of life at all levels of society. These rituals are all performed toward perishable goals and thus can never satisfy the inner need of the soul. This movement constitutes a movement in ignorance which leads to further ignorance. While religious rituals are also in the realm of human activity, if performed with growing levels of understanding and devotion toward the Divine, they will lead to greater and greater peace and self-knowledge. If one goes to a church simply to fulfill some custom or out of guilt there will be little benefit and slow growth in spirituality. Therefore, the Sages and Saints have enjoined several rituals, prayers and words of power to help spiritual aspirants turn their minds toward spiritual realization rather than toward perishable worldly attainments which will inevitably lead to disappointments, pain and sorrow. In this journey, a spiritual preceptor who can point the way toward true spiritual realization is needed, otherwise spiritual practice becomes a drudgery or empty formality which will not purify and transform the human heart.

Goddess Worship and Rituals of Enlightenment

You should observe a set of rituals whenever you intend to practice any form of meditation. These will gradually help to settle the mind even before you actually sit to practice the meditation. They are especially useful if you are a busy person or if you have many thoughts or worries on the mind. First take a bath. Water is the greatest cleanser of impurities. In ancient times the Temple complexes included a sacred lake for bathing. Practitioners of yoga would bathed before entering the temples and engaging in the mystery rituals such as those presented in this volume.

Once you have bathed, put on clothing which you have specifically reserved for the practice of meditation. This will have a strong effect on your mind and will bring meditative vibrations to you because the clothing will retain some of the subtle essence of the meditation experience each time you use them. The clothing should be loose and comfortable. 100% Cotton or Silk is recommended because they are natural materials which will allow the skin to breath and should not cause allergic reactions. Keep the clothing clean and use the same clothing for your meditation practice.

When you are ready, go to your special room or corner which you have set aside for meditation. Take the phone off the hook or turn off the ringer and close the door behind you, leaving instructions not to be disturbed for the period of time you have chosen. When you sit for meditation, light a candle and some incense of your choice and then choose a comfortable position maintaining the back straight, either sitting on the floor in the cross-legged posture (Lotus), sitting in a chair with feet on the floor or lying on your back on the floor in the corpse-mummy pose (without falling asleep). If possible, use a sistrum, bell or other noise making device before and after uttering the following prayers.

Procedure

1- Traditionally, the ritual begins with the winter solstice (around Dec. 22), continues through the birth of Heru which is celebrated on December 25th, and concludes on Dec. 26th. In addition to this a ceremony has been included with the rising of Sopdu for optimum auspiciousness on December 31st. However, these rituals may be carried out on any day of the year and will provide positive benefits if the mystical symbolism of the rituals is reflected upon. The ritual may be performed by a single person or in a group.

2- The following procedure is to be observed each day of the ritual.
   A- Fasting: Do not eat anything between 6 PM and 7 am during each day of the ritual beginning Dec. 21. Vegetarian diet is to be observed always.
   B- Celibacy, non-violence, truthfulness, in thought, word and deed are to be observed during each day of the ritual.
   C- Go to bed by 11 PM and commence the ritual at 6 am every day, facing the eastern horizon.
   D- On December 31st the ritual is to be carried out at 11 PM facing the southern pole.
   E- The epic story of the Ausarian Resurrection along with the various aspects of the Goddess are to be read and studied each day.

83

Mysticism of the Ancient Egyptian Goddess

F- Recite the hekau of the Goddess as prescribed.

Articles necessary for the ritual: Ankh, Water, Bread, Noise making device, Candle, Incense, Icon.

1- **Ankh** - ☥ A metal Ankh may be used but even an image on a piece of paper will do. The Ankh is one of the most universal symbols expressing eternal life, the union of opposites and it was, and still is used by the world religious traditions (Ancient Egyptian religion, early Christianity, Indian religion and others.

2- **Water** - A water libation vessel ⩜ or a simple cup will do. Water symbolizes the flow of Creation as well as its very essence. It refers to the Primeval Ocean wherein all is formless and pure as well as the very life sustaining essence of Creation. In ancient times the Nile river served as a source of life and spiritual energy. In this last aspect it is likened to the blood of the Divine (Blood of Asar, Blood of Christ, etc.) Today, the river Jordan, the Ganges and other rivers are viewed in the same light.

3- **Bread** - ☷, Bread symbolizes the physical nature, the solid, concrete and visible portion of Creation. In mystical terms it is the body of the Divinity. Throughout the ceremony, the water and bread are glorified. A portion is given to the earth as a libation and another portion is consumed at the end of the ceremony as a communion with the Divine.

4- **Candle** - The candle holds deep mystical symbolism. It contains within itself all of the four elements of Creation: fire, earth (wax in solid form), water (wax in liquefied form), and air. All are consumed in the burning process and all of them come together to produce light. This singular light represents the singular consciousness which shines throughout the entire universe. This light is the illumination which causes life to exist and it is the reason and source of the human mind. This light is life itself and life is the Divinity. Therefore, the Supreme Self is ever-present in the candle, in the universe (nature) and in your heart and mind.

5- **Noise making device** - ♀ sistrum, tambourine, drum, cymbals, bells. One of these will be sufficient. The noise making device symbolizes the awakening of the heart from the delusion of ignorance. Use the device wherever you see the sistrum symbol ♀. The sistrum is one of the most important symbols of the Goddess as she stirs up the gross elements within the body and the dull intellect so as to instill wisdom and enlightenment.

In reference to the iconography surrounding Aset, in the spiritual struggle against Set, there is one important artifact which was used at the time of uttering prayers and recitations. This is the *Sistrum*. The sistrum is commonly known as the rattle of Aset or Hetheru (both are aspects of the same goddess principle). The sistrum consists of a handle surmounted by a metal hoop through which four pieces of metal rods are set. When shaken, the rods hit against the loop (see below) and cause a distinctive sound. The sistrum was produced in two forms. The second form incorporated the figure of the *Naos* or shrine (Holy of Holies) of the goddess instead of a loop. Plutarch, the ancient Greek writer, wrote about the sistrum and its spiritual significance:

"The Sistrum also shows that existent things must be shaken up and never have cessation from impulse, but as it were, be wakened when they fall asleep and die away.

For they say they turn aside and beat off Typhon [Set] with sistra, corruption binds nature fast and brings her to a stand. The Sistrum frees her and raises her from death by means of motion. Now the sistrum has a curved top, and its arch contains the four [things]. For the part of the cosmos which is subject to generation is circumscribed to the sphere of the moon, and all [things] in it are moved and changed by the four elements - fire and earth and water and air.

And on the arch of the sistrum, at the top, they put the metal figure of a cat with a human face and at the bottom, below the shaken things, the face sometimes of Aset and sometimes of Nebthet, - symbolizing by the faces generation and consummation (for these are the changes and motions of the elements.

The Ancient Egyptian name of the sistrum is *skhem* or *sesheshet*. The goddess or priestess who holds and plays the sistrum to the Divine is known as *Neter sesheshet*. The *hoop* is a symbol of the *world-encircling* orbit of the moon. The sistrum often has two faces of Hetheru. The two faces of Hetheru represent Aset and Nebthet or life and death, respectively, the opposites of Creation. The four metal rods represent the elements, but also the four spiritual energy centers of the spiritual body known as the pillar of Asar. The human body, the energy which causes it to live and the subtle substance which composes the thoughts in the human mind, are all made up of minute particles of the elements. The mystical meaning of the shaking up of the rattle refers to the shaking up of human consciousness from the evil of ignorance and complacency which leads to spiritual stagnation and the development of evil (sinful-Setian) flaws in the human character (anger, hatred, greed, selfishness, lust, elation, depression, etc.). This process further relates to awakening the mind to the futility of trying to satisfy the desires of the lower nature, the fallacy of vanity and egoism, and the fleeting nature of happiness which is gained through and is dependent on worldly attainments or achievements. Further, the sistrum refers to realizing the transient and relative nature of human existence and the discovery of a higher vision wherein the Divine is to be recognized and experienced. It means, moving from ignorance to true knowledge, and from the pain of human suffering to the glory of divine inspiration and abiding happiness.

The Sistrum may be likened to the *Conch* in Indian mystical symbolism, and the hand held Buddhist prayer wheel, as they are used for the same purpose, to "churn the ethers" in order to stir up the latent spiritual energies which lead to spiritual enlightenment. Other cultures may use bells, cymbals or other hand held objects to accomplish the same effect.

6- **Incense**. Incense invokes divine awareness through the sense of smell. When you perform spiritual practices and use a special incense consistently, every time that you smell the incense you will have divine thoughts and feelings even if you are not in the regular area of meditation. Therefore, select a fragrance which appeals to you and reflect within yourself that this is the fragrance of your Higher Self in the same way as a flower emanates fragrance. Visualize that you are smelling Divinity itself.

7- **Icon** - spiritual Image. A sculpture, picture or other symbol of a Deity (as a symbol of the Supreme Being). In keeping with the Goddess theme choose a form of the Ancient Egyptian female Divinity, otherwise you may choose an Ancient Egyptian deity such as Heru, Asar, etc., or a Christian icon such as Jesus or Mary, or an Eastern icon such as Buddha (Buddhist), or Krishna, Rama or Saraswati of the Vedantic-Hindu tradition, etc. Choose an icon according to your spiritual inclination, one which engenders a feeling of love and devotion within you. This will help you to develop devotion towards the Divine which will hasten your progress in yoga. When the Divine image or symbol is used it is called worship of the Supreme Being with name and form. As you progress you will be instructed on how to worship the Divine in an abstract way without using any names or forms.

Observances:

"They who revere MAAT are *long lived*;
they who are covetous have no tomb."

Ancient Egyptian Proverb

During this special period of time of the Mother Worship festivity you should try to uphold the following observances in order to gain the greatest benefit from the ritual. These observances are to be considered as your offerings or sacrifices to the Goddess.

Goddess Worship and Rituals of Enlightenment

Firstly, give the offering of study time to the Goddess Aset (Aset). In the form of *Rekhat* she is the mistress of wisdom. Therefore you must sacrifice some time for studying and reflecting upon the wisdom teachings. In doing so you open the way for increasing levels of understanding and communion with the Divine. However, it is not enough to just study the teachings. You must also practice them day by day. You must sacrifice your negative qualities to the goddess. Whenever you feel anger, hatred, greed, conceit, covetousness, lust, selfishness, etc., and become aware of these, put forth self-effort to sublimate the negative qualities and offer them to the Goddess. Request that it (they) be removed from your heart and that understanding and forgiveness (for yourself as well as the other person) be put in its place. These negative qualities are the true source of your sorrow in life and the reason why the higher vision of eternity is blocked from your view. Therefore, with earnestness, seek the blessings of the Goddess and work towards attaining the light of wisdom which removes all pain and misery and bestows the knowledge of immortality and the bliss of Divine realization.

As a special offering to Maat you should observe the teachings of virtue and order. Strive to remain in balance in all things. This includes your work, entertainment, food, sleep, etc. "Keeping the balance" is one of the most important ways to promote peace, harmony and an atmosphere which is conducive to learning and spiritual enlightenment. If you are constantly engaged in extremes like arguing too much, partying too much, or working too much, all of these have a negative effect on the mind and body because they drain the mental power and leave worldly impressions in the unconscious. Entertainment is supposed to relax your mind. However, if you overindulge you will find that you will become dependent on the entertainment and will feel drained by it afterward. It works this way for all things. Therefore, strive to be balanced in all of your activities. Do not engage in arguments, avoid the company of extreme people, extreme violence in life as well as in TV or movies. Also avoid elation; becoming overly happy is in reality not normal. It is an abnormal reaction to something which makes you feel good. Elation ultimately leads to depression. So try to avoid undue anxiety, worry, euphoria or intoxication of any kind. When adversity arises, see it as a test from the Goddess. She is giving you an opportunity to practice controlling your mind and giving her prominence, rather than your personal desires and egoistic feelings. Put down your petty feelings of revenge or resentment and accept your discomfort as an austerity. Avoid positive as well as negative extremes. If you succeed in keeping the balance, the Goddess bestows the blessings of inner peace and contentment. Those who indulge in belligerence and a fighting nature receive the curse of never-ending mental unrest and adversity in life.

Thirdly, if you give presents during this time of festivity, do so without expectations. Give without reservations and attachments and do not expect anything in return. The *Fetters* or negative qualities in the human heart develop out of the lower need to have and hold objects as sources of pleasure, to feel praise from others and to gain material success, believing that material success brings happiness. Spiritual wisdom shows that these things cannot bring true happiness. True happiness comes from understanding that you are not just a human personality caught in a rat race to hoard objects. Do you know of anyone who is truly happy? Even those who are billionaires are not immune from disappointments, failed marriages, mental and physical illnesses, suicide and all of the other adversities of life. The idea that happiness comes from material success, possessions, relationships, passion, sexuality or fame is in reality a grave error which leads people to untold sufferings and disappointments in this lifetime as well as future ones. Therefore, seek a deeper basis of happiness by discovering your true identity as the Higher Self which transcends the lower forms of human happiness. Seek to discover the peace and happiness which is not dependent on objects, relationships or material success and which transcends these. As you keep these observances you are in reality sacrificing the egoistic values, the Setian lower self within you, the evil of ignorance which is keeping you in bondage to the lower feelings and negativity, anger, envy and unhappiness which are preventing you from experiencing Divine inspiration and awareness of the Divine presence.

Commencement

Begin by sounding the noise making device Ψ and then reciting the following auspicious hekau-words of power for commencing your spiritual practice. Each prayer should be recited four times. This quadruplicate format is a symbolic way to propitiate the divine forces which control the four quarters of the phenomenal universe and the heavenly realms. There are four directions (North, South, East, and West) which the mind is aware of in the physical plane as in the astral. The prayer is directed towards the purification of the mind and body which will allow your spiritual practice (movement) to be unobstructed in earth as well as in heaven. It is a propitiation to the Divine that you should not be confined to the temporal world of time and space, and physical body and ego-self consciousness, so that you may go beyond the ignorance of ordinary human existence and thereby discover the truth of your true nature as one with the Supreme Self.

Aset says: "I Aset, am all that has been, all that is, or shall be; and no mortal man hath ever unveiled me."

Invoke the presence of Aset-Maat-Nebthet, the embodiment of wisdom and devotion toward the Divine. Aset (Aset) is the mother of the universe and she herself veils her true form, as the Supreme Transcendental Self. This "veil" of ignorance is only due to illusion. Therefore, pray to Aset to make her presence known in her true form. This "unveiling" is a metaphor symbolizing the intuitional revelation of the Divine or Enlightenment in your mind. The Divine is already present in your heart. Aset is in your heart and only needs to be revealed. However, she can only reveal herself to the true aspirant, one who is devoted to her (the Self) and her alone.

The original rubric of this ritual prescribes that the following verses be sung in the temple of ASAR KHENTI AMENTIU, the Great God, the Lord of Abtu, on the 22nd to the 26th days of the fourth month of the season AKHU (December) by two priestesses and a priest (symbolizing the presence of Aset, Nebthet and Asar). These women were to be virgins, and ceremonially pure; their bodies were shaved and they wore garlands of ram's hair and held tambourines in their hands. On the shoulders of one was written the name **ASET** and on the shoulders of the other **NEBTHET**. All were to be celibate. The chanting begins:

𓊽𓏤

Goddess Worship and Rituals of Enlightenment

Dua Aset
(Adorations to Aset)
Dua Aset
Dua Aset
Dua Aset

Dua Maat
(Adorations to Maat)
Dua Maat
Dua Maat
Dua Maat

Dua Nebt-het
(Adorations to Nebthet)
Dua Nebt-het
Dua Nebt-het
Dua Nebt-het

Dua Asar
("Hail lord ASAR,)
Dua Asar
Dua Asar
Dua Asar

"Glory be to Asar Un-nefer, the great god within Abydos, king of eternity, lord of the everlasting.
"Glory be to Asar Un-nefer, the great god within Abydos, king of eternity, lord of the everlasting.
"Glory be to Asar Un-nefer, the great god within Abydos, king of eternity, lord of the everlasting.
"Glory be to Asar Un-nefer, the great god within Abydos, king of eternity, lord of the everlasting.

Beautiful Youth, come to thy house at once; we see thee not.
Hail, Beautiful Boy, come to thy house, draw near after thy separation from us.
Hail, Beautiful Youth, pilot of time, who groweth except at his hour.
Holy Image of his father Tenn[1], mysterious essence proceeding from ATEM[2]

The Lord, the Lord! how much more wonderful is he than his father, the first-born son of the womb of his mother. Come thou back to us in thy actual form; we will embrace thee. Depart not from us, thou Beautiful Face, dearly beloved one, The Image of Tenn, Male, Master of lovejoys. Come thou in peace, our lord, we would see thee. Thy two sisters will join together thy members[3] , no pain shall touch thee, they will make the injury to thee to be as if it had never happened. Our heads are turned backwards. Great Mighty One among the gods, the road which thou travellest cannot be described.

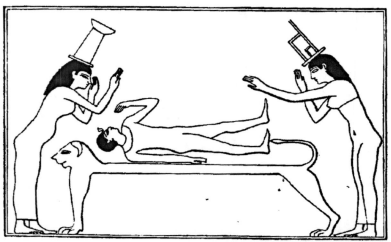

Aset and Nebthet cry over the body of Asar
(Relief from the Temple of Aset)

The Babe, the Child at morning and at evening, except when thou encirclest the heavens and the earth with bodily form.
Thou art the Bull of the Two Sisters[4]. Come, thou, Babe, growing young when setting, our Lord, we would see thee,
Come thou in peace, Babe Great of his father, thou art established in thy house.
Fear not, thy son Heru avengeth thee.
NEKA[5] shall be carried off and thrust in his cavern of fire every day; his name shall be hacked to pieces among all the gods; TEBHA[6] shall become stinking corruption.
Thou art in thy house; fear not. SUT[7] is suffering all the evil which he hath committed; what NUT sent hath speared him.[8]
Come, Youth of the Saffron[9] -colored Face, thou ONE who growest young, whose two eyes[10] are beautiful.

I am thy sister Aset, the darling of thy heart. Because of my love for thee, thou being absent, I water the earth with my tears this day.

(Libation: pour some water on the ground)

Goddess Worship and Rituals of Enlightenment

Whilst thou travellest thou art hymned by us, and life springeth up for us out of thy nothingness[11]. O our Lord, come in peace, let us see thee. Hail, Prince, come in peace, drive away the fire[12] which is in our houses.

Hail, Bull of those in AMENTI[13], ONE, immovable, how much more marvelous than the gods is the Babe, the Male, the mighty heir of GEBB,[14] who was born God among gods.

Come thou to thy Two Widows. The whole of the Company of the gods and goddesses encircle thee that they may repulse SET —cursed be his name!—when he cometh behind the shrine before thy father RA, who shooteth out [fire] and repulseth the SEBAU devils.

Come, thy kinsfolk await thee; drive away sorrow from our houses.
Come, thy kinsfolk await thee; there is none more stable than thee, O dweller in solitude.

The throne of our Lord is in peace. The Victor, he is greater than his long-suffering when the Lock fiend alighteth on his enemies.

O Soul who does live again, the two sisters unite thy members.
I hid myself among the bushes[15] to conceal thy son that he might answer for thee, for separation from thee was a time of sore distress. Did she[16] not gather up thy members? I went on alone, I crept round about among the vegetation. A very large crocodile came after thy son-(a female with the face of a male)-but I knew, and ANPU; and I went round and retraced my way for my brother leaping clear from the evil one.

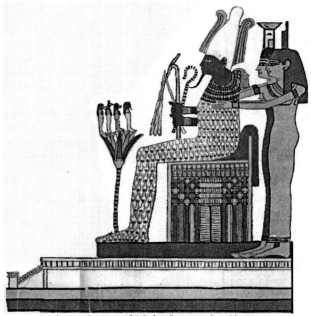

Asar, Aset and Nebethet in the Shrine

Hail, Beautiful Boy, come to thy exalted house, thy exalted house; let thy back be to thy house. The gods are upon their thrones. Hail I Come in peace, KING. Come in peace. Thy son Heru is avenging thee. Thou causest great grief to thy Two Queens, we weep for thee at thy shrines. Babe! How lovely it is to see thee! Come, come to us, O great one, glorify our love. Come thou to thy house, fear not.

> O ye gods who are in heaven.
> O ye gods who are on the earth.
> O ye gods who are in the Duat (Underworld).
> O ye gods who are in the abyss.
> O ye gods who are in the service of the deep.
> We follow the lord, the lord of love.

I traverse the roads that thy love may come to me. I fly over the earth. I rest not in seeking thee. A flame of thy love is to me.
The perfume of thy body is [that of] PUNT[17].
The Cow[18] weeps for thee with her voice. She avengeth thee.
She sets thy nose on thy face, she collects thy bones for thee.
Thy mother NUT cometh to thee with holy offerings. She builds thee up with the life of her body. Thou art endowed with soul, thou art endowed with soul. Thou art established, thou art established.

Thy hair is turquoise on thy body when thou enter the fields of turquoise. Thy hair is lapis-lazuli[19]; thou art more lapis-lazuli than thy hair. Thy skin and limbs are alabaster of the south. Thy bones are silver. Thy teeth are turquoise, or the unguent of thy hair is liquid *anti*[20] (myrrh). Thy skull is lapis-lazuli.

Presentation of Art-Heru

Instruction:

Receive this Eye of Heru by approaching the Spiritual Preceptor. He or she will utter the following invocation.

May Life, Stability and Contentment be yours!

The recipient replies:

Nuk pu Heru, Nuk pu Heru
Conclusion

Instruction: After the reading remain in silent meditation for ten minutes or as long as you like. You may mentally chant the hekau of your choice or practice concentration on the Divine form. Some suggested hekau are included below.

Om Asar Aset Heru
The Divine Self, Om and the three forms,
the Divine Trinity Asar, Aset and Heru.

Om Aset
The Divine Self, Om and the Divine Goddess form, Aset.

Nuk pu Ast (Aset)
I am Aset

Nuk pu Asar
I am Asar

Nuk pu NETER
I am the Supreme Divinity.

End: With upraised arms give thanks to the Goddess and invoke the hekau of purity.

Adorations to Aset
Adorations to Maat
Adorations to Nebthet

I am pure. I am pure. I am Pure. I am Pure.

I have washed my front parts with the waters of libations, I have cleansed my hinder parts with drugs which make wholly clean, and my inward parts have been washed in the liquor of Maat.

ANNUAL GODDES WORSHIP FOR DECEMBER 31st

For the special occasion on the last day of the festivity, plan for a special area out of doors on December 31 to carry out the ritual if possible. While the Mother Worship and Meditation ritual presented here is designed to be carried out on New Year's Eve, it may effectively be used as a means of daily worship every evening, especially when the star Sopdu is rising.

Aset and Sopdu

A significant correlation between Ancient Egyptian and modern Christian mythology is the Christian myth surrounding the Three Kings who traveled to the site of the birth of Jesus. In ancient times the star Sopdu was held to be especially important in Egyptian culture and religion because its rising announced the coming of the New Year and the flooding of the Nile river which was the source of all sustenance.

The name Sopdu comes from the Greek *Seirios*, "scorching". Sopdu is the brightest star in the sky, situated in the constellation Canis Major. It is located at a distance of 8.7 light years (51 trillion miles) from our earth, which makes it one of the closest and brightest stars. Also, she (Sopdu) is visible from all over the earth. Sopdu consists of a binary star system which includes Sopdu (Sirius) and Sopdu B (Digitaria). Sopdu B is a white dwarf star. The largest known stars are called super giants with diameters that may be more than 400 times that of our sun. The small stars which are known as white dwarfs may have diameters that can be only 0.01 times that of our sun.

This *Sothic Period* is based on the period by which the Earth's Solar system circulates around the star Sopdu. This period of time consists of approximately 1,461 years. There is an elaborate mythology associated with Sopdu wherein the Ancient Egyptians and the present day Dogon peoples of West Africa have used Sopdu as a basis for mythic teachings as well as the reckoning of time. One Ancient Egyptian myth which the Dogon peoples have adopted is that the gods and goddesses originated in Sopdu and came to the earth. There are astronomical indications that the earth's solar system and Sopdu, together, are part of a larger solar system composed of the three stars. This indicates a different cosmology than that which is currently taught by modern science, and it explains the ancient Creation myths which incorporate Sopdu as a source for life on earth. In ancient times, all acts were dated according to the vague year, composed of exactly 360 days plus the five epagomenal days consecrated to the *Neters*: Asar, Aset, Seth, Nebthet and Heru.

Many Ancient Egyptian temples were constructed in such a way that the light of Sopdu reached the inner chambers. The Ancient Egyptian name of Sopdu is *Sept*, △₀★, or *Sopdu*. Its symbols are related to Aset and are sometimes used in her name, ★◯ ₀𝕁, or to refer to her. There are three stars in the Sahu constellation which point almost directly to Sopdu which rises in the eastern sky. Sopdu is associated with

Aset, the mother of Heru. Thus, the three Kings in the Christian myth relate to the light of the three stars in the constellation of Sahu which travels toward the rising light of salvation (Sopdu) which is being born on the winter solstice. In ancient times, Heru was considered as the Savior, who was born from the Goddess Aset. In the Christian era, Aset became the prototype of Mary, the mother of Jesus and Jesus assumed the role which had been held by Heru from ancient times. In modern times, the star Sopdu is still held in high regard by the Dogon nation of Mali in Africa. Sopdu is a companion star to our sun. Our solar system and Sopdu revolve around each other, both revolve around the Milky Way galaxy and the Milky Way revolves around the universe. One myth surrounding Sopdu is that human souls originate there and return there after death.

$$\bigstar\bigstar\bigstar \qquad\qquad \bigstar$$

From a mystical perspective, the three stars in Sahu's Belt refer to the Trinity principle which pervaded the entire system of Ancient Egyptian mythology. The Supreme Being, *Nebertcher*, is known as the One who expresses as Three, , "I became from God one, gods three". Three here refers to the three states of consciousness (waking, dream and dreamless deep sleep), the three modes of operation of human mind (subject, object and the relationship between the two*), and the three modes of Creation: consciousness, mind and matter or Heaven, ÿuat (Duat) and Earth. The triad or Trinity emanates from the singular source or essence of Creation, the Supreme Being, who is transcendent of the three. Thus, *one* symbolizes the Supreme, transcendental Divinity and the *three* symbolize the multiplicity of Creation which is at all times sustained by divine will. Thus, the three follow the one. This principle of the *three* is also present in the annunciation scene from the temple of Luxor, Egypt, and was assimilated into the mythology of Jesus Christ with the three kings who went to see the new born child, Jesus. (*see *The Ausarian Resurrection* and the *Egyptian Yoga Guide Book Series* for more information)

New Years Eve is an especially important time in reference to the mysticism of Sopdu. A little known fact about Sopdu is that on New Years Eve, Sopdu rises to the apex of the meridian above the earth and can be seen directly above from anywhere in the world at the midnight hour. Thus, Sopdu marks the beginning (birth) of a New Year as well as the continuing cycle of life which reminds us of the glory and precision of the universe. Thus, in this aspect Sopdu is a supreme example of Aset as the mother who gives birth to Heru and also in her aspect as Maat, the universal order of Creation. Therefore, this time offers a great opportunity to reflect upon the attributes and teachings of Aset, Heru and Maat. The Ancient Egyptian Pyramid Texts* explain that the rising of Sopdu and the birth of the New Year is synonymous with the resurrection of the initiate who is Asar and whose spiritual seed rises in the form of Heru, the vindicator, the renewed spirit (enlightenment).

Goddess Worship and Rituals of Enlightenment

The passage in the Pyramid Texts is relating the birth of Heru, the spirit of Asar, through Aset. It is very important to understand that *The Asar* being referred to in the Pyramid Texts as well as the *Egyptian Book of Coming Forth By Day* is in reality the initiate, you. Therefore, as you read about Asar, keep in mind that it is you who are being renewed, you who are being reborn.

Instruction: On December 31st the ritual, as described in the previous section of Mother Worship, should be carried out at 11 PM. At midnight all readings should be concluded and meditation on Aset-Maat-Nebthet (Aset-Maat-Nebthet) in the form of Sopdu is to begin. Sopdu may be found by facing due south. Next look at the southern horizon and then look up, midway between the horizon and the zenith (the part of the sky that is directly overhead). You will see the brightest star in the area and that will be Sopdu. Just to the right you will see three stars. These are known as the belt of Sahu.

Attunement with the Cosmic Energies of Supdu

REFLECTIONS ON USHET REKHAT

The study and worship of the Divine Mother is one of the most effective paths to practice mystical spirituality. The very basis of the program of worship is an understanding that Asar, the Soul, has been dismembered and it is the Goddess who reconstitutes his body and who provides the nourishment and nursing which is required to bring the Spirit back to life. You will notice that the supplication in the ritual is a beckoning directed both at Asar and at Heru. This is because Asar and Heru are in reality one and the same. The resurrection of Asar is synonymous with the birth of Heru. The birth of Heru is synonymous with the vindication and resurgence of Asar. This task of bringing Asar back to life, the Goddess achieves by providing her own body, wisdom and love. Thus, the spiritual aspirant is to see himself or herself as the Goddess who is giving the body, mind and soul to the Spirit. In being part of the ritual and by observing the teachings imparted by it, every participant draws from these qualities and engenders the birth of the Spirit, Heru, within themselves.

The way for the birth of the Spirit is opened by practicing the teachings. The Spirit cannot emerge if there are setian qualities in control of the mind. Setian qualities are the demoniac attributes of those who are devoid of virtue. These are: ignorance, elation, depression, desire, selfishness, greed, hatred, lust, etc. These are the means by which Set dismembers the body of Asar. The demoniac qualities are overcome with virtuous qualities. These include truthfulness, honesty, moderation, study of the teachings, meditation, prayer, selfless service, forgiveness, forbearance, bearing insults, non-violence, etc. All of these virtues are to be practiced not only outwardly but more importantly, with introspection and honesty. They are to be practiced in thought, word and deed. Only when they are practiced internally can there be true inner purification. If you do not harm others but maintain ill will against them you will not become a vessel for Divine inception. Instead, you will be a conduit for negativity and sinfulness and the teachings and rituals will remain as external factors and will not touch your heart. These virtues and spiritual practices are the means by which the spiritual body is reconstituted and made whole again so that it becomes a container, fit to carry the essence of the Divine.

Therefore, as you practice the ritual and teachings throughout the year and reflect on your progress, you should ask yourself if you are becoming slower to anger? Are you gaining a deeper understanding of the wisdom teachings? Are you growing in devotion to the Divine? Are you discovering a deeper inner peace and contentment? Is it becoming easier to hold onto your positive thoughts about the world and your life? You will discover that as time passes on you are gaining an increased awareness of the presence of the Divine, and a great peace and joy are becoming part of every aspect of your life.

May the Goddess Lead You To Discover
The Blessings of Her Divine Essence.

NOTES on the ritual of Ushet Rekhat:

1- An ancient god of Creation.

2- The god of the setting sun.

3- Referring to Aset and Nebthet and the dismemberment of Asar which was perpetrated by Set.

4- Aset and Nebthet.

5- A devil.

6- A devil. The allusion to the name being hacked up is a reference to the understanding that the name of a person is a part of their very being. To kill the name was equivalent to killing its owner; the name was the being.

7- Set or the leader of the devils.

8- One myth related to the Ausarian Resurrection tells of how Set swallowed the crescent moon, which symbolizes the resurrection of Asar and the growth of Heru, but the Sky-goddess Nut speared him and made him vomit the moon.

9- a-The dried orange-yellow stigmas of a kind of crocus, used to color and flavor food and as a dye. b- An orange-yellow.

10- The eyes of Heru, the sun and moon, also symbolizing the union of individual and cosmic consciousness. (see *Egyptian Yoga: The Philosophy of Enlightenment* and the *Egyptian Yoga Guide Series*)

11- This deepest and most dark realm of the Duat is Asar, Himself, and this is why Asar is referred to as the "Lord of the Perfect Black" and is often depicted as being black or green of hue. It is also why Nut, Aset, and Hetheru are also described as "dark-skinned". They are emanations from this realm of blackness which is described as a void or "*nothingness*" in the hieroglyphic papyrus entitled *The Laments of Aset and Nebthet*. This notion of nothingness is akin to the Buddhist notion of *Shunya* or the "void", which refers to the area of consciousness which is devoid of mental concepts and thoughts. When there are no thoughts or forms in the mind, it is calm, expansive and peaceful. When there are thoughts in the mind, the mental awareness is narrowed and defined in terms of concepts. If the mind is confined to these concepts and narrow forms of thought, then it is confined to that which is limited and temporal. If it eradicates its desires, cravings and illusions, then it becomes aware of the innermost reality and realizes its connection to the entire cosmos. Thus, the teaching of the Duat (Amentet, Re-Stau, etc.) gives insight into the nature of the human mind. It is a description of the mental landscape, its demons (everything that leads to ignorance and mental agitation), and gods and goddesses who represent the positive thoughts, feelings and the way to discover the abode of the innermost Self (everything that leads to peace, harmony and wisdom). Therefore, the task of a spiritual aspirant is to eradicate the concepts, agitation, desires and cravings in the mind and to discover the "hidden" innermost reality which is Hetep (Supreme Peace), eternal and pure. (*from an inscription in the temple of Denderah, Egypt)

From a higher level of understanding, the Duat is the unconscious mind and Asar is that level which transcends the thinking processes... its deepest region. It is the level of consciousness that is experienced during deep dreamless sleep. Therefore, it is the "Hidden" aspect of the human heart, and thus, it is also known as Amun.

12- In mystical philosophy there are two forms in which fire is used as a symbol. One of these is the fire of wisdom which burns away ignorance and establishes self-knowledge. This is the fire which Ra and his Eye in the form of the Udjat or in the form of Hetheru, represents. The second form of symbolism likens the feeling to a hell-fire which is experienced due to separation from the Divine. This is why the entire litany of this text is based on supplications by Aset and Nebthet who are propitiating for the return of Asar-Heru. They are paving the way for the return by means of their devotional love, which is backed up by action. They do not just pray and supplicate but are also clearing the way, reconstructing the body of Asar, protecting it from evil and also by providing their hearts as a place for the birth of the spirit of Asar in the form of Heru.

13- Amenti is the "Other World", the "Hidden" realm of Asar known as the Netherworld or astral world or "Tuat". Asar presides here as judge of the dead and Aset presides as the essence of the Amenti in her form or aspect as Amentet.

14- Gebb is the husband of Nut and father of Asar, Aset, Set and Nebthet.

15- This is an allusion to the plight of Aset when she hid in the papyrus swamps of the Nile after Set had killed Asar and wanted to capture her and kill Heru.
16- A reference to Aset herself in the third person (i.e. "I")
17- The spice land.
18- Aset
19- Special blue color.
20- Myrrh.

Index

Goddess Worship and Rituals of Enlightenment

Other Books From C M Books

P.O.Box 570459
Miami, Florida, 33257
(305) 378-6253 Fax: (305) 378-6253

This book is part of a series on the study and practice of Ancient Egyptian Yoga and Mystical Spirituality based on the writings of Dr. Muata Abhaya Ashby. They are also part of the Egyptian Yoga Course provided by the Sema Institute of Yoga. Below you will find a listing of the other books in this series. For more information send for the Egyptian Yoga Book-Audio-Video Catalog or the Egyptian Yoga Course Catalog.

Now you can study the teachings of Egyptian and Indian Yoga wisdom and Spirituality with the Egyptian Yoga Mystical Spirituality Series. The Egyptian Yoga Series takes you through the Initiation process and lead you to understand the mysteries of the soul and the Divine and to attain the highest goal of life: ENLIGHTENMENT. The *Egyptian Yoga Series*, takes you on an in depth study of Ancient Egyptian mythology and their inner mystical meaning. Each Book is prepared for the serious student of the mystical sciences and provides a study of the teachings along with exercises, assignments and projects to make the teachings understood and effective in real life. The Series is part of the Egyptian Yoga course but may be purchased even if you are not taking the course. The series is ideal for study groups.

Prices subject to change.

Prices subject to change.

1.   EGYPTIAN YOGA: THE PHILOSOPHY OF ENLIGHTENMENT An
        original, fully illustrated work, including hieroglyphs, detailing the meaning of
        the Egyptian mysteries, tantric yoga, psycho-spiritual and physical exercises.
        Egyptian Yoga is a guide to the practice of the highest spiritual philosophy
        which leads to absolute freedom from human misery and to immortality. It is
        well known by scholars that Egyptian philosophy is the basis of Western and

Goddess Worship and Rituals of Enlightenment

Middle Eastern religious philosophies such as *Christianity, Islam, Judaism,* the *Kabala,* and Greek philosophy, but what about Indian philosophy, Yoga and Taoism? What were the original teachings? How can they be practiced today? What is the source of pain and suffering in the world and what is the solution? Discover the deepest mysteries of the mind and universe within and outside of your self. 8.5" X 11" ISBN: 1-884564-01-1 Soft $19.95

2.   EGYPTIAN YOGA II: The Supreme Wisdom of Enlightenment by Dr. Muata Ashby ISBN 1-884564-39-9 $23.95 U.S. In this long awaited sequel to *Egyptian Yoga: The Philosophy of Enlightenment* you will take a fascinating and enlightening journey back in time and discover the teachings which constituted the epitome of Ancient Egyptian spiritual wisdom. What are the disciplines which lead to the fulfillment of all desires? Delve into the three states of consciousness (waking, dream and deep sleep) and the fourth state which transcends them all, Neberdjer, "The Absolute." These teachings of the city of Waset (Thebes) were the crowning achievement of the Sages of Ancient Egypt. They establish the standard mystical keys for understanding the profound mystical symbolism of the Triad of human consciousness.

3.   THE KEMETIC DIET: GUIDE TO HEALTH, DIET AND FASTING Health issues have always been important to human beings since the beginning of time. The earliest records of history show that the art of healing was held in high esteem since the time of Ancient Egypt. In the early 20th century, medical doctors had almost attained the status of sainthood by the promotion of the idea that they alone were "scientists" while other healing modalities and traditional healers who did not follow the "scientific method' were nothing but superstitious, ignorant charlatans who at best would take the money of their clients and at worst kill them with the unscientific "snake oils" and "irrational theories". In the late 20th century, the failure of the modern medical establishment's ability to lead the general public to good health, promoted the move by many in society towards "alternative medicine". Alternative medicine disciplines are those healing modalities which do not adhere to the philosophy of allopathic medicine. Allopathic medicine is what medical doctors practice by an large. It is the theory that disease is caused by agencies outside the body such as bacteria, viruses or physical means which affect the body. These can therefore be treated by medicines and therapies The natural healing method began in the absence of extensive technologies with the idea that all the answers for health may be found in nature or rather, the deviation from nature. Therefore, the health of the body can be restored by correcting the aberration and thereby restoring balance. This is the area that will be covered in this volume. Allopathic techniques have their place in the art of healing. However, we should not forget that the body is a grand achievement of the spirit and built into it is the capacity to maintain itself and heal itself. Ashby, Muata ISBN: 1-884564-49-6 $28.95

4.   INITIATION INTO EGYPTIAN YOGA Shedy: Spiritual discipline or program, to go deeply into the mysteries, to study the mystery teachings and literature profoundly, to penetrate the mysteries. You will learn about the mysteries of initiation into the teachings and practice of Yoga and how to become an Initiate of the mystical sciences. This insightful manual is the first in a series which introduces you to the goals of daily spiritual and yoga practices: Meditation, Diet, Words of Power and the ancient wisdom teachings. 8.5" X 11" ISBN 1-884564-02-X   Soft Cover $24.95 U.S.

5.   *THE AFRICAN ORIGINS OF CIVILIZATION, MYSTICAL RELIGION AND YOGA PHILOSOPHY* HARD COVER EDITION ISBN: 1-884564-50-X $80.00 U.S.   81/2" X 11"   Part 1, Part 2, Part 3 in one volume 683 Pages Hard Cover First Edition Three volumes in one. Over the past several years I have been asked to put together in one volume the most important evidences showing the correlations and common teachings between Kamitan (Ancient Egyptian) culture and religion and that of India. The questions of the history of Ancient Egypt, and the latest archeological evidences showing civilization and culture in Ancient Egypt and its spread to other countries, has intrigued many scholars as well as mystics over the years. Also, the possibility that Ancient Egyptian Priests and Priestesses migrated to Greece, India and other countries to carry on the traditions of the Ancient Egyptian Mysteries, has been speculated over the years as well. In chapter 1 of the book *Egyptian Yoga The Philosophy of Enlightenment,* 1995, I first introduced the deepest comparison between Ancient Egypt and India that had been brought forth up to that time. Now, in the year 2001 this new book, *THE AFRICAN ORIGINS OF CIVILIZATION, MYSTICAL RELIGION AND YOGA PHILOSOPHY,* more fully explores the motifs, symbols and philosophical correlations between Ancient Egyptian and Indian mysticism and clearly shows not only that Ancient Egypt and India were connected culturally but also spiritually. How does this knowledge help the spiritual aspirant? This discovery has great importance for the Yogis and mystics who follow the philosophy of Ancient Egypt and the mysticism of India. It means that India has a longer history and heritage than was previously understood. It shows that the mysteries of Ancient Egypt were essentially a yoga tradition which did not die but rather developed into the modern day systems of Yoga technology of India. It further shows that African culture developed Yoga Mysticism earlier than any other civilization in history. All of this expands our understanding of the unity of culture and the deep legacy of Yoga, which stretches into the distant past, beyond the Indus Valley civilization, the earliest known high culture in India as well as the Vedic tradition of Aryan culture. Therefore, Yoga culture and mysticism is the oldest known tradition of spiritual development and Indian mysticism is an extension of the Ancient Egyptian mysticism. By understanding the legacy which Ancient Egypt gave to India the mysticism of India is better understood and by comprehending the heritage of Indian Yoga, which is rooted in Ancient Egypt the Mysticism of Ancient Egypt is also better understood. This expanded understanding allows us to prove the underlying kinship of humanity, through the common symbols, motifs and

philosophies which are not disparate and confusing teachings but in reality expressions of the same study of truth through metaphysics and mystical realization of Self. (HARD COVER)

6. AFRICAN ORIGINS BOOK 1 PART 1 African Origins of African Civilization, Religion, Yoga Mysticism and Ethics Philosophy-Soft Cover $24.95 ISBN: 1-884564-55-0

7. AFRICAN ORIGINS BOOK 2 PART 2 African Origins of Western Civilization, Religion and Philosophy(Soft) -Soft Cover $24.95 ISBN: 1-884564-56-9

8. EGYPT AND INDIA (AFRICAN ORIGINS BOOK 3 PART 3) African Origins of Eastern Civilization, Religion, Yoga Mysticism and Philosophy-Soft Cover $29.95 (Soft) ISBN: 1-884564-57-7

9. THE MYSTERIES OF ISIS: **The Ancient Egyptian Philosophy of Self-Realization** - There are several paths to discover the Divine and the mysteries of the higher Self. This volume details the mystery teachings of the goddess Aset (Isis) from Ancient Egypt- the path of wisdom. It includes the teachings of her temple and the disciplines that are enjoined for the initiates of the temple of Aset as they were given in ancient times. Also, this book includes the teachings of the main myths of Aset that lead a human being to spiritual enlightenment and immortality. Through the study of ancient myth and the illumination of initiatic understanding the idea of God is expanded from the mythological comprehension to the metaphysical. Then this metaphysical understanding is related to you, the student, so as to begin understanding your true divine nature. ISBN 1-884564-24-0 $22.99

10. EGYPTIAN PROVERBS: TEMT TCHAAS *Temt Tchaas* means: collection of ——Ancient Egyptian Proverbs How to live according to MAAT Philosophy. Beginning Meditation. All proverbs are indexed for easy searches. For the first time in one volume, ——Ancient Egyptian Proverbs, wisdom teachings and meditations, fully illustrated with hieroglyphic text and symbols. EGYPTIAN PROVERBS is a unique collection of knowledge and wisdom which you can put into practice today and transform your life. 5.5"x 8.5" $14.95 U.S   ISBN: 1-884564-00-3

11. THE PATH OF DIVINE LOVE The Process of Mystical Transformation and The Path of Divine Love   This Volume focuses on the ancient wisdom teachings of "Neter Merri" –the Ancient Egyptian philosophy of Divine Love and how to use them in a scientific process for self-transformation. Love is one of the most powerful human emotions. It is also the source of Divine feeling that unifies God and the individual human being. When love is fragmented and diminished by egoism the Divine connection is lost. The Ancient tradition of Neter Merri leads human beings back to their Divine connection, allowing them

to discover their innate glorious self that is actually Divine and immortal. This volume will detail the process of transformation from ordinary consciousness to cosmic consciousness through the integrated practice of the teachings and the path of Devotional Love toward the Divine. 5.5"x 8.5" ISBN 1-884564-11-9 $22.99

12. INTRODUCTION TO MAAT PHILOSOPHY: Spiritual Enlightenment Through the Path of Virtue   Known as Karma Yoga in India, the teachings of MAAT for living virtuously and with orderly wisdom are explained and the student is to begin practicing the precepts of Maat in daily life so as to promote the process of purification of the heart in preparation for the judgment of the soul. This judgment will be understood not as an event that will occur at the time of death but as an event that occurs continuously, at every moment in the life of the individual. The student will learn how to become allied with the forces of the Higher Self and to thereby begin cleansing the mind (heart) of impurities so as to attain a higher vision of reality. ISBN 1-884564-20-8 $22.99

13. MEDITATION The Ancient Egyptian Path to Enlightenment   Many people do not know about the rich history of meditation practice in Ancient Egypt. This volume outlines the theory of meditation and presents the Ancient Egyptian Hieroglyphic text which give instruction as to the nature of the mind and its three modes of expression. It also presents the texts which give instruction on the practice of meditation for spiritual Enlightenment and unity with the Divine. This volume allows the reader to begin practicing meditation by explaining, in easy to understand terms, the simplest form of meditation and working up to the most advanced form which was practiced in ancient times and which is still practiced by yogis around the world in modern times. ISBN 1-884564-27-7 $24.99

14. THE GLORIOUS LIGHT MEDITATION Technique of Ancient Egypt ISBN: 1-884564-15-1$14.95 (PB) New for the year 2000. This volume is based on the earliest known instruction in history given for the practice of formal meditation. Discovered by Dr. Muata Ashby, it is inscribed on the walls of the Tomb of Seti I in Thebes Egypt. This volume details the philosophy and practice of this unique system of meditation originated in Ancient Egypt and the earliest practice of meditation known in the world which occurred in the most advanced African Culture.

15. THE SERPENT POWER: The Ancient Egyptian Mystical Wisdom of the Inner Life Force.   This Volume specifically deals with the latent life Force energy of the universe and in the human body, its control and sublimation. How to develop the Life Force energy of the subtle body. This Volume will introduce the esoteric wisdom of the science of how virtuous living acts in a subtle and mysterious way to cleanse the latent psychic energy conduits and vortices of the spiritual body. ISBN 1-884564-19-4 $22.95

Goddess Worship and Rituals of Enlightenment

16.   EGYPTIAN YOGA *The Postures of The Gods and Goddesses* Discover the physical postures and exercises practiced thousands of years ago in Ancient Egypt which are today known as Yoga exercises. This work is based on the pictures and teachings from the Creation story of Ra, The Asarian Resurrection Myth and the carvings and reliefs from various Temples in Ancient Egypt 8.5" X 11" ISBN 1-884564-10-0 Soft Cover $21.95   Exercise video $20

17.   EGYPTIAN TANTRA YOGA: The Art of Sex Sublimation and Universal Consciousness This Volume will expand on the male and female principles within the human body and in the universe and further detail the sublimation of sexual energy into spiritual energy. The student will study the deities Min and Hathor, Asar and Aset, Geb and Nut and discover the mystical implications for a practical spiritual discipline. This Volume will also focus on the Tantric aspects of Ancient Egyptian and Indian mysticism, the purpose of sex and the mystical teachings of sexual sublimation which lead to self-knowledge and Enlightenment. 5.5"x 8.5" ISBN 1-884564-03-8 $24.95

18.   ASARIAN RELIGION: RESURRECTING OSIRIS The path of Mystical Awakening and the Keys to Immortality NEW REVISED AND EXPANDED EDITION! The Ancient Sages created stories based on human and superhuman beings whose struggles, aspirations, needs and desires ultimately lead them to discover their true Self. The myth of Aset, Asar and Heru is no exception in this area. While there is no one source where the entire story may be found, pieces of it are inscribed in various ancient Temples walls, tombs, steles and papyri. For the first time available, the complete myth of Asar, Aset and Heru has been compiled from original Ancient Egyptian, Greek and Coptic Texts. This epic myth has been richly illustrated with reliefs from the Temple of Heru at Edfu, the Temple of Aset at Philae, the Temple of Asar at Abydos, the Temple of Hathor at Denderah and various papyri, inscriptions and reliefs. Discover the myth which inspired the teachings of the *Shetaut Neter* (Egyptian Mystery System - Egyptian Yoga) and the Egyptian Book of Coming Forth By Day. Also, discover the three levels of Ancient Egyptian Religion, how to understand the mysteries of the Duat or Astral World and how to discover the abode of the Supreme in the Amenta, *The Other World* The ancient religion of Asar, Aset and Heru, if properly understood, contains all of the elements necessary to lead the sincere aspirant to attain immortality through inner self-discovery. This volume presents the entire myth and explores the main mystical themes and rituals associated with the myth for understating human existence, creation and the way to achieve spiritual emancipation - *Resurrection.* The Asarian myth is so powerful that it influenced and is still having an effect on the major world religions. Discover the origins and mystical meaning of the Christian Trinity, the Eucharist ritual and the ancient origin of the birthday of Jesus Christ. Soft Cover ISBN: 1-884564-27-5 $24.95

19.   THE EGYPTIAN BOOK OF THE DEAD MYSTICISM OF THE PERT EM HERU $28.95   ISBN# 1-884564-28-3 Size: 8½" X 11" I Know myself, I

know myself, I am One With God!–From the Pert Em Heru "The Ru Pert em Heru" or "Ancient Egyptian Book of The Dead," or "Book of Coming Forth By Day" as it is more popularly known, has fascinated the world since the successful translation of Ancient Egyptian hieroglyphic scripture over 150 years ago. The astonishing writings in it reveal that the Ancient Egyptians believed in life after death and in an ultimate destiny to discover the Divine. The elegance and aesthetic beauty of the hieroglyphic text itself has inspired many see it as an art form in and of itself. But is there more to it than that? Did the Ancient Egyptian wisdom contain more than just aphorisms and hopes of eternal life beyond death? In this volume Dr. Muata Ashby, the author of over 25 books on Ancient Egyptian Yoga Philosophy has produced a new translation of the original texts which uncovers a mystical teaching underlying the sayings and rituals instituted by the Ancient Egyptian Sages and Saints. "Once the philosophy of Ancient Egypt is understood as a mystical tradition instead of as a religion or primitive mythology, it reveals its secrets which if practiced today will lead anyone to discover the glory of spiritual self-discovery. The Pert em Heru is in every way comparable to the Indian Upanishads or the Tibetan Book of the Dead." Muata Abhaya Ashby

20. ANUNIAN THEOLOGY THE MYSTERIES OF RA The Philosophy of Anu and The Mystical Teachings of The Ancient Egyptian Creation Myth Discover the mystical teachings contained in the Creation Myth and the gods and goddesses who brought creation and human beings into existence. The Creation Myth holds the key to understanding the universe and for attaining spiritual Enlightenment. ISBN: 1-884564-38-0 40 pages $14.95

21. MYSTERIES OF MIND Mystical Psychology & Mental Health for Enlightenment and Immortality based on the Ancient Egyptian Philosophy of Menefer -Mysticism of Ptah, Egyptian Physics and Yoga Metaphysics and the Hidden properties of Matter. This volume uncovers the mystical psychology of the Ancient Egyptian wisdom teachings centering on the philosophy of the Ancient Egyptian city of Menefer (Memphite Theology). How to understand the mind and how to control the senses and lead the mind to health, clarity and mystical self-discovery. This Volume will also go deeper into the philosophy of God as creation and will explore the concepts of modern science and how they correlate with ancient teachings. This Volume will lay the ground work for the understanding of the philosophy of universal consciousness and the initiatic/yogic insight into who or what is God? ISBN 1-884564-07-0 $22.95

22. THE GODDESS AND THE EGYPTIAN MYSTERIESTHE PATH OF THE GODDESS THE GODDESS PATH The Secret Forms of the Goddess and the Rituals of Resurrection The Supreme Being may be worshipped as father or as mother. *Ushet Rekhat* or *Mother Worship*, is the spiritual process of worshipping the Divine in the form of the Divine Goddess. It celebrates the most important forms of the Goddess including *Nathor, Maat, Aset, Arat, Amentet and Hathor*

Goddess Worship and Rituals of Enlightenment

and explores their mystical meaning as well as the rising of *Sirius,* the star of Aset (Aset) and the new birth of Hor (Heru). The end of the year is a time of reckoning, reflection and engendering a new or renewed positive movement toward attaining spiritual Enlightenment. The Mother Worship devotional meditation ritual, performed on five days during the month of December and on New Year's Eve, is based on the Ushet Rekhit. During the ceremony, the cosmic forces, symbolized by Sirius - and the constellation of Orion ---, are harnessed through the understanding and devotional attitude of the participant. This propitiation draws the light of wisdom and health to all those who share in the ritual, leading to prosperity and wisdom. $14.95 ISBN 1-884564-18-6

23. *THE MYSTICAL JOURNEY FROM JESUS TO CHRIST* $24.95   ISBN# 1-884564-05-4 size: 8½" X 11" Discover the ancient Egyptian origins of Christianity before the Catholic Church and learn the mystical teachings given by Jesus to assist all humanity in becoming Christlike. Discover the secret meaning of the Gospels that were discovered in Egypt. Also discover how and why so many Christian churches came into being. Discover that the Bible still holds the keys to mystical realization even though its original writings were changed by the church. Discover how to practice the original teachings of Christianity which leads to the Kingdom of Heaven.

24. THE STORY OF ASAR, ASET AND HERU: An Ancient Egyptian Legend (For Children)   Now for the first time, the most ancient myth of Ancient Egypt comes alive for children. Inspired by the books *The Asarian Resurrection: The Ancient Egyptian Bible* and *The Mystical Teachings of The Asarian Resurrection, The Story of Asar, Aset and Heru* is an easy to understand and thrilling tale which inspired the children of Ancient Egypt to aspire to greatness and righteousness.   If you and your child have enjoyed stories like *The Lion King* and *Star Wars you will love The Story of Asar, Aset and Heru.* Also, if you know the story of Jesus and Krishna you will discover than Ancient Egypt had a similar myth and that this myth carries important spiritual teachings for living a fruitful and fulfilling life. This book may be used along with *The Parents Guide To The Asarian Resurrection Myth: How to Teach Yourself and Your Child the Principles of Universal Mystical Religion.* The guide provides some background to the Asarian Resurrection myth and it also gives insight into the mystical teachings contained in it which you may introduce to your child. It is designed for parents who wish to grow spiritually with their children and it serves as an introduction for those who would like to study the Asarian Resurrection Myth in depth and to practice its teachings. 41 pages   8.5" X 11"   ISBN: 1-884564-31-3 $12.95

25. THE PARENTS GUIDE TO THE AUSARIAN RESURRECTION MYTH: How to Teach Yourself and Your Child the Principles of Universal Mystical Religion.   This insightful manual brings for the timeless wisdom of the ancient through the Ancient Egyptian myth of Asar, Aset and Heru and the mystical teachings contained in it for parents who want to guide their children to

understand and practice the teachings of mystical spirituality. This manual may be used with the children's storybook *The Story of Asar, Aset and Heru* by Dr. Muata Abhaya Ashby. 5.5"x 8.5"   ISBN: 1-884564-30-5 $14.95

26.   HEALING THE CRIMINAL HEART BOOK 1 Introduction to Maat Philosophy, Yoga and Spiritual Redemption Through the Path of Virtue   Who is a criminal? Is there such a thing as a criminal heart? What is the source of evil and sinfulness and is there any way to rise above it? Is there redemption for those who have committed sins, even the worst crimes?   Ancient Egyptian mystical psychology holds important answers to these questions. Over ten thousand years ago mystical psychologists, the Sages of Ancient Egypt, studied and charted the human mind and spirit and laid out a path which will lead to spiritual redemption, prosperity and Enlightenment.   This introductory volume brings forth the teachings of the Asarian Resurrection, the most important myth of Ancient Egypt, with relation to the faults of human existence: anger, hatred, greed, lust, animosity, discontent, ignorance, egoism jealousy, bitterness, and a myriad of psycho-spiritual ailments which keep a human being in a state of negativity and adversity. 5.5"x 8.5"   ISBN: 1-884564-17-8 $15.95

27.   THEATER & DRAMA OF THE ANCIENT EGYPTIAN MYSTERIES: Featuring the Ancient Egyptian stage play-"The Enlightenment of Hathor' Based on an Ancient Egyptian Drama, The original Theater -Mysticism of the Temple of Hetheru $14.95   By Dr. Muata Ashby

28.   GUIDE TO PRINT ON DEMAND: SELF-PUBLISH FOR PROFIT, SPIRITUAL FULFILLMENT AND SERVICE TO HUMANITY Everyone asks us how we produced so many books in such a short time. Here are the secrets to writing and producing books that uplift humanity and how to get them printed for a fraction of the regular cost. Anyone can become an author even if they have limited funds. All that is necessary is the willingness to learn how the printing and book business work and the desire to follow the special instructions given here for preparing your manuscript format. Then you take your work directly to the non-traditional companies who can produce your books for less than the traditional book printer can. ISBN: 1-884564-40-2 $16.95 U. S.

29.   Egyptian Mysteries: Vol. 1, Shetaut Neter ISBN: 1-884564-41-0 $19.99 What are the Mysteries? For thousands of years the spiritual tradition of Ancient Egypt, *Shetaut Neter,* "The Egyptian Mysteries," "The Secret Teachings," have fascinated, tantalized and amazed the world. At one time exalted and recognized as the highest culture of the world, by Africans, Europeans, Asiatics, Hindus, Buddhists and other cultures of the ancient world, in time it was shunned by the emerging orthodox world religions. Its temples desecrated, its philosophy maligned, its tradition spurned, its philosophy dormant in the mystical *Medu Neter*, the mysterious hieroglyphic texts which hold the secret symbolic meaning that has scarcely been discerned up to now. What are the secrets of *Nehast* {spiritual awakening and emancipation, resurrection}. More than just a

literal translation, this volume is for awakening to the secret code *Shetitu* of the teaching which was not deciphered by Egyptologists, nor could be understood by ordinary spiritualists. This book is a reinstatement of the original science made available for our times, to the reincarnated followers of Ancient Egyptian culture and the prospect of spiritual freedom to break the bonds of *Khemn,* "ignorance," and slavery to evil forces: *Sáaa* .

30.   EGYPTIAN MYSTERIES VOL 2: Dictionary of Gods and Goddesses ISBN: 1-884564-23-2 $21.95 This book is about the mystery of neteru, the gods and goddesses of Ancient Egypt (Kamit, Kemet). Neteru means "Gods and Goddesses." But the Neterian teaching of Neteru represents more than the usual limited modern day concept of "divinities" or "spirits." The Neteru of Kamit are also metaphors, cosmic principles and vehicles for the enlightening teachings of Shetaut Neter (Ancient Egyptian-African Religion). Actually they are the elements for one of the most advanced systems of spirituality ever conceived in human history. Understanding the concept of neteru provides a firm basis for spiritual evolution and the pathway for viable culture, peace on earth and a healthy human society.   Why is it important to have gods and goddesses in our lives? In order for spiritual evolution to be possible, once a human being has accepted that there is existence after death and there is a transcendental being who exists beyond time and space knowledge, human beings need a connection to that which transcends the ordinary experience of human life in time and space and a means to understand the transcendental reality beyond the mundane reality.

31.   EGYPTIAN MYSTERIES VOL. 3 The Priests and Priestesses of Ancient Egypt ISBN: 1-884564-53-4 $22.95 This volume details the path of Neterian priesthood, the joys, challenges and rewards of advanced Neterian life, the teachings that allowed the priests and priestesses to manage the most long lived civilization in human history and how that path can be adopted today; for those who want to tread the path of the Clergy of Shetaut Neter.

32.   THE KING OF EGYPT: The Struggle of Good and Evil for Control of the World and The Human Soul ISBN 1-8840564-44-5 $18.95   This volume contains a novelized version of the Asarian Resurrection myth that is based on the actual scriptures presented in the Book Asarian Religion (old name – Resurrecting Osiris). This volume is prepared in the form of a screenplay and can be easily adapted to be used as a stage play. Spiritual seeking is a mythic journey that has many emotional highs and lows, ecstasies and depressions, victories and frustrations. This is the War of Life that is played out in the myth as the struggle of Heru and Set and those are mythic characters that represent the human Higher and Lower self. How to understand the war and emerge victorious in the journey o life? The ultimate victory and fulfillment can be experienced, which is not changeable or lost in time. The purpose of myth is to convey the wisdom of life through the story of divinities who show the way to

overcome the challenges and foibles of life. In this volume the feelings and emotions of the characters of the myth have been highlighted to show the deeply rich texture of the Ancient Egyptian myth. This myth contains deep spiritual teachings and insights into the nature of self, of God and the mysteries of life and the means to discover the true meaning of life and thereby achieve the true purpose of life. To become victorious in the battle of life means to become the King (or Queen) of Egypt.Have you seen movies like The Lion King, Hamlet, The Odyssey, or The Little Buddha? These have been some of the most popular movies in modern times. The Sema Institute of Yoga is dedicated to researching and presenting the wisdom and culture of ancient Africa. The Script is designed to be produced as a motion picture but may be addapted for the theater as well. $19.95   copyright 1998 By Dr. Muata Ashby

33.   AFRICAN DIONYSUS: FROM EGYPT TO GREECE: The Kamitan Origins of Greek Culture and Religion ISBN: 1-884564-47-X $24.95 U.S. FROM EGYPT TO GREECE   This insightful manual is a reference to Ancient Egyptian mythology and philosophy and its correlation to what later became known as Greek and Rome mythology and philosophy. It outlines the basic tenets of the mythologies and shoes the ancient origins of Greek culture in Ancient Egypt. This volume also documents the origins of the Greek alphabet in Egypt as well as Greek religion, myth and philosophy of the gods and goddesses from Egypt from the myth of Atlantis and archaic period with the Minoans to the Classical period. This volume also acts as a resource for Colleges students who would like to set up fraternities and sororities based on the original Ancient Egyptian principles of Sheti and Maat philosophy. ISBN: 1-884564-47-X $22.95 U.S.

34.   THE FORTY TWO   PRECEPTS OF MAAT,   THE PHILOSOPHY OF RIGHTEOUS ACTION AND THE   ANCIENT EGYPTIAN WISDOM TEXTS ADVANCED STUDIES This manual is designed for use with the 1998 Maat Philosophy Class conducted by Dr. Muata Ashby. This is a detailed study of Maat Philosophy. It contains a compilation of the 42 laws or precepts of Maat and the corresponding principles which they represent along with the teachings of the ancient Egyptian Sages relating to each. Maat philosophy was the basis of Ancient Egyptian society and government as well as the heart of Ancient Egyptian myth and spirituality. Maat is at once a goddess, a cosmic force and a living social doctrine, which promotes social harmony and thereby paves the way for spiritual evolution in all levels of society. ISBN: 1-884564-48-8 $16.95 U.S.

Music Based on the Prt M Hru and other Kemetic Texts

Available on Compact Disc $14.99 and Audio Cassette $9.99

Adorations to the Goddess

Music for Worship of the Goddess

NEW Egyptian Yoga Music CD
by Sehu Maa
Ancient Egyptian Music CD
Instrumental Music played on reproductions of Ancient Egyptian
Instruments– Ideal for <u>meditation</u> and
reflection on the Divine and for the practice of spiritual programs and
<u>Yoga exercise sessions.</u>

©1999 By Muata Ashby
CD $14.99 –

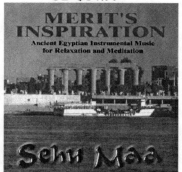

MERIT'S INSPIRATION
NEW Egyptian Yoga Music CD

Mysticism of the Ancient Egyptian Goddess

by Sehu Maa
Ancient Egyptian Music CD
Instrumental Music played on
reproductions of Ancient Egyptian Instruments– Ideal for <u>meditation</u> and
reflection on the Divine and for the practice of spiritual programs and
<u>Yoga exercise sessions.</u>
©1999 By
Muata Ashby
CD $14.99 –
UPC# 761527100429

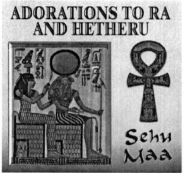

ANORATIONS TO RA AND HETHERU
NEW Egyptian Yoga Music CD
By Sehu Maa (Muata Ashby)
Based on the Words of Power of Ra and HetHeru
played on reproductions of Ancient Egyptian Instruments **Ancient
Egyptian Instruments used: Voice, Clapping, Nefer Lute, Tar Drum,
Sistrums, Cymbals** – The Chants, Devotions, Rhythms and Festive
Songs Of the Neteru – Ideal for meditation, and devotional singing and
dancing.
©1999 By Muata Ashby
CD $14.99 –
UPC# 761527100221

Goddess Worship and Rituals of Enlightenment

SONGS TO ASAR ASET AND HERU
NEW
Egyptian Yoga Music CD
By Sehu Maa

played on reproductions of Ancient Egyptian Instruments– The Chants,
Devotions, Rhythms and
Festive Songs Of the Neteru - Ideal for meditation, and devotional singing and dancing.
Based on the Words of Power of Asar (Asar), Aset (Aset) and Heru (Heru) Om Asar Aset
Heru is the third in a series of musical explorations of the Kemetic
(Ancient Egyptian) tradition of music. Its ideas are based on the Ancient
Egyptian Religion of Asar, Aset and Heru and it is designed for listening,
meditation and worship. ©1999 By Muata Ashby
CD $14.99 –
UPC# 761527100122

HAARI OM: ANCIENT EGYPT MEETS INDIA IN MUSIC
NEW Music CD
By Sehu Maa

The Chants, Devotions, Rhythms and

Festive Songs Of the Ancient Egypt and India, harmonized and played on reproductions of ancient instruments along with modern instruments and beats. Ideal for meditation, and devotional singing and dancing.

Haari Om is the fourth in a series of musical explorations of the Kemetic (Ancient Egyptian) and Indian traditions of music, chanting and devotional spiritual practice. Its ideas are based on the Ancient Egyptian Yoga spirituality and Indian Yoga spirituality.

©1999 By Muata Ashby

CD $14.99 –

UPC# 761527100528

RA AKHU: THE GLORIOUS LIGHT
NEW
Egyptian Yoga Music CD
By Sehu Maa

The fifth collection of original music compositions based on the Teachings and Words of The Trinity, the God Asar and the Goddess Nebethet, the Divinity Aten, the God Heru, and the Special Meditation Hekau or Words of Power of Ra from the Ancient Egyptian Tomb of Seti I and more... played on reproductions of Ancient Egyptian Instruments and modern instruments - Ancient Egyptian Instruments used: Voice, Clapping, Nefer Lute, Tar Drum, Sistrums, Cymbals

— The Chants, Devotions, Rhythms and Festive Songs Of the Neteru – Ideal for meditation, and devotional singing and dancing.

©1999 By Muata Ashby

CD $14.99 –

UPC# 761527100825

GLORIES OF THE DIVINE MOTHER
Based on the hieroglyphic text of the worship of Goddess Net.
The Glories of The Great Mother
©2000 Muata Ashby
CD $14.99 UPC# 761527101129`

Mysticism of the Ancient Egyptian Goddess

Order Form

Telephone orders: Call Toll Free: 1(305) 378-6253. Have your AMEX, Optima, Visa or MasterCard ready.

Fax orders: 1-(305) 378-6253   E-MAIL ADDRESS: Semayoga@aol.com

Postal Orders: Sema Institute of Yoga, P.O. Box 570459, Miami, Fl. 33257. USA.

Please send the following books and / or tapes.

ITEM

_____ Cost $_____

_____ Cost $_____

_____ Cost $_____

_____ Cost $_____

_____ Cost $_____

Total $_____

Name:_____

Physical Address:_____

City:_____ State:_____ Zip:_____

Sales tax: Please add 6.5% for books shipped to Florida addresses

_____Shipping: $6.50 for first book and .50¢ for each additional

_____Shipping: Outside US $5.00 for first book and $3.00 for each additional

_____Payment:_____

_____Check -Include Driver License #:

_____

_____Credit card: _____ Visa, _____ MasterCard, _____ Optima,

_____ AMEX.

Card number:_____

Name on card:_____ Exp. date:_____/_____

431785

Made in the USA